Unlocking
God's
Supernatural Zone

Unlocking God's Supernatural Zone

THE ATMOSPHERE OF FAITH FOR MIRACLES

Evan. Muthu

Copyright © 2017 by Evan. Muthu.

ISBN: Softcover 978-1-5434-1662-6
eBook 978-1-5434-1661-9

All rights reserved. No part of this book may be reproduced or transmitted in any form or by any means, electronic or mechanical, including photocopying, recording, or by any information storage and retrieval system, without permission in writing from the copyright owner.

Scripture quotations marked KJV are from the Holy Bible, King James Version (Authorized Version). First published in 1611. Quoted from the KJV Classic Reference Bible, Copyright © 1983 by The Zondervan Corporation.

Any people depicted in stock imagery provided by Thinkstock are models, and such images are being used for illustrative purposes only.
Certain stock imagery © Thinkstock.

Print information available on the last page.

Rev. date: 05/02/2017

To order additional copies of this book, contact:
Xlibris
1-888-795-4274
www.Xlibris.com
Orders@Xlibris.com
742718

CONTENTS

1) Gift of the Kingdom 1
2) You Shall Receive Power 8
3) Stepping Into the Miraculous 17
4) Then Came the Glory 36
5) Secret Place of the Most High 52
6) Touch of Heaven 67
7) Over Flowing River 78
8) The 7 Facets of God's Spirit 92
9) Contending for Breakthrough.... 108
10) Receiving and Releasing 121

Foreword

Come! Let us experience Jesus together! Let us see His Glory and smell the sweetness of His presence, let us hear His voice as he speaks ever so gently calling us unto Himself. Then as a result of getting to know Him, learning of Him and spending time with Him we will see Jesus in action in the lives of those most needing His touch and deliverance.

Everywhere Jesus walked He left the footprints of His presence in the lives of those He touched. Jesus has not changed! He is still the same! The only difference is that now, just as He did after Pentecost, He continues His walking and working through those who personally know Him in the power of His Holy Spirit and know Him by name. Bro Muthu is a humble servant of Messiah who knows Jesus in His person and His works. Here, in this book, this man of God lends you his insight into the wonderful workings of Jesus and what only He can do for the hurting and hopeless. Bro Muthu knows JESUS, lives and breaths JESUS and most of all, shares JESUS with those he meets, wherever it might be in the world.

I have had the privilege of getting to know Bro. Muthu and his lovely family over the past several years that we have been working in and out of Malaysia. He is the real deal! There is no pretence in him, he loves JESUS and people and brings the two together in his ministry. He and his wife Susan are fearless, faithful servants of the LORD. They truly walk with Him and know Him. Like the Psalmist said of Moses, **"He made known his ways unto Moses, his acts unto the children of Israel."** Psalm 103:7 The children of Israel merely saw the acts of God through Moses, but Moses himself knew and understood God's ways. He knew God himself by name, and knew Him by encounter after encounter. Moses' face glowed with the Glory of the I AM because he was "endued and endowed" with His presence. Such is Bro Muthu. The acts of God that flow through this man are the result of him knowing and spending time with JESUS. Just as it was said of Peter and John in Acts 4:13 it can be said of Bro. Muthu and Sis. Susan, **"…and they took knowledge of them, that they had been with Jesus."**

In the following pages you will not only be blessed by the many wonderful testimonies of God's power that transforms lives, situations and circumstances, but you will experience JESUS and His personal presence in your life and hear His voice as he calls you into a deeper place in Him, into the **Supernatural Zone**, into the **atmosphere of Faith** for the miraculous.

Monte Showalter,
Inter-Regional Missionary Evangelist &
International Coordinator of Global Campus Ministries

Many wonder if Ephesians 4 is still valid for today. Do we still see Apostolic ministry in action? Does God still do signs and wonders?

Hear and be amazed at the modern day Apostolic ministry of a man and woman God has called to show forth His power in these last days. No, not usually in large stadiums or venues, but in the most remote corners of the world where very few are willing to go. The jungles and mountains of Northeast India and Nepal, treacherous terrain, dubious bridges over rushing mountain rivers - none of these conditions deter Brother Muthu and his wife from fulfilling the call God has placed on their lives.

Why would they leave the comforts of a modern city like Kuala Lumpur to preach in places most of us have never heard of? It is the Gospel of Jesus Christ that compels them...a taking of the Gospel to the uttermost parts of the earth. Because he was saved from Hinduism through the miraculous display of God's power in healing his mother from cancer, Brother Muthu now goes forth with great faith declaring the works of God that are still in effect today. Signs, wonders and miracles are common in their ministry and thousands have experienced their personal Pentecost through the efforts of Brother Muthu and Sister Susan

Read, be challenged and believe God will do something for you as you read their story.

Brother Allan Shalm
Missionary to Pakistan, Malaysia & Asia

When prayer becomes our lifestyle, the supernatural becomes the natural.

The words of Luke written in Acts 17: 27- 28 create a hunger in our souls to follow the examples of those before us:

> *"[27] That they should seek the LORD, if haply they might feel after him, and find him, though he be not far from every one of us:*
>
> *[28] For in him we live, and move, and have our being; ..."*

As we seek Him, we find Him! He is very near; He is in us! No better words can be used to express our continual dependency than the words "in him."

I trust that this book will help you understand that God's power is available for all who will submit to His will and follow Him. Rev. Muthu, and his wife, Susan, exemplify lifestyles of seeking Him, of living "in him," and a ministry that "moves" with Him. May these written testimonials of His supernatural power create a deep hunger and thirst in your soul for a more intimate lifestyle with Him, and may these pages be a reminder that "all things are possible!"

Roger D. Buckland
Regional Director/Pacific

God planted Abraham in an unfriendly wilderness and at the same time, HE planted the church in a lost world. Both had the same goal, to prepare them for a Kingdom, not of this world. He authorized and anointed His disciples to cross all borders, province or princedom, to preach good news to the poor, to proclaim deliverance to the captives and recovery of sight to the blind, and to release the oppressed.

To all the missionaries, evangelists, pastors, leaders, ministers and saints that have labored and laboring in the field with a true burden of SOULS, He did give this command.

Acknowledgement

I wish to thank my Wife Susana who has been my life partner, friend, encourager, strength and co-minister in the mission field and stood alongside in the ministry for the past 28 years and to my three lovely princesses Suanne, Venice & Joy. God brought them as gifts and blessings to our lives and the ministry.

> For, the LORD is
> my strength and song:
> He also has become
> my salvation.
> Isaiah;12:22

Preface

The purpose of this book is to enable every believer, saint and leader of the gospel to recognize and unlock the potential and authority they possess inside of them through the Holy Spirit. Every incident and story written is an actual encounter of heaven touching the earth in the lives of people through the power of the Spirit of God to the nations we have been travelling for the past 17 years. May this book be a strength and encouragement to you and tnlock the doors to your spiritual conquest for a deeper relation and walk with the One who has called you out the darkness to his marvelous light.

Jesus said to His disciples just before He ascended up to heaven, "Ye shall receive power, after that the Holy Ghost is come upon you: and ye shall be witnesses unto me" Act 1:8. On the day of Pentecost as the Holy Spirit descended on the 120 of them not only did they receive the infilling of the spirit as part of God's plan for Salvation but they also received power which is the reminder of John the Baptist sayings 'I baptize you with water for repentance, but after me will come One mightier than I, whose sandals I am not worthy to carry. He will baptize you with the Holy Spirit and with fire.

Indeed in the Acts experience, it was a baptism of the spirit with fire and it tells of the witnessing of these Spirit-filled disciples, the Lord working with them, and confirming the word with signs following.

Our Jesus is just the same as he was two thousand years ago, the anointing is just the same. The Pentecostal experience is just the same, and we are to seek and desire those things that shook the world through the hands of twelve ordinary men. His first disciples followed Him just when He signaled. It was just Him, not what He did for them, no money, no honor, and no place. It wasn't healing either.

Take Levi, for example, a customs tax official.

Sitting collecting tax dues, a shadow fell across his desk and he looked up, straight into the eyes of Jesus as He simply said "Follow me!" Captivated, he dropped everything. He knew nothing about Jesus being the Messiah, but this was the living word that stood before him, greater than religion, larger than the Jewish customs and Larger than any prophet that walked on the earth before. The disciples learn one secret, just one secret to be a beam of the glory of Jesus, through the fellowship of his suffering and stepping into his resurrection power. Without Jesus, we can do nothing. Without His genuine anointing, our ministry is nothing but sounding brass and a tinkling cymbal.

John the Baptist said concerning Jesus, "He shall baptize you with the Holy Ghost, and with fire." God's ministers are to be a flame of fire - a perpetual flame, a constant fire, a continual burning, burning and shining lights. God has nothing less for us than to be flames. We must have a living faith in God, a faith that God's great might and power may flame through us until our whole life is energized by the power of God and the fire of God.

The anointing of the Holy Spirit is given through people to demonstrate God's love and power. Christ means the "Anointed One". Because Christ is in us the same anointing that He had on earth we also have.

(Luke 4:18-19 NKJV) "The Spirit of the LORD is upon me, because He has anointed me to preach the Gospel to the poor; He has sent me to heal the brokenhearted, to proclaim liberty to the captives and recovery of sight to the blind, To set at liberty those who are oppressed; {19} To proclaim the acceptable year of the LORD."

The 5 results of the Anointing

1. The anointing is given to preach the Gospel to the poor.
2. The anointing is given to heal and restore people.
3. The anointing is given to proclaim freedom to the captives from every bondage.
4. The anointing is given to open blind eyes.
5. The anointing is given to set people free.

The anointing is given to preach the Gospel to the poor, to bring the revelation of God's love, His deity and salvation to those who are seeking.

God's anointing flows to those who are hungry for a touch from His Spirit. The anointing has less to do with the person that it flows through than it does with the person who receives it, and the One who sent it, God Almighty.

When the Holy Spirit comes, He comes to enable us to show forth the revelation of who Jesus Christ is in all His glory, to make Him known as the One who saves, redeems and heals today as in the days of the apostles. The Baptism of the Spirit is to enable us preach the good news to the poor, proclaim deliverance to the captives and recovery of sight to the blind, to release the oppressed, as they did at the beginning, through the power of the Holy Spirit sent down from heaven and with the manifestation of the gifts of the Spirit.

God has brought us to a new order of things, a life of victory and overcoming beyond every comprehension of human mind. This overcoming state will only be embraced through walking in the spirit constantly. A person who has been fully saturated with the presence of the spirit will clearly have an understanding of his mission in the kingdom of God.

1 GIFT OF THE KINGDOM

COL 1:13
Who hath delivered us from the power of darkness, and hath translated us into the kingdom of his dear Son.

The pressing need of the hour today, as believers we should be burning and shining forth God's light to reflect the glory of the resurrection Jesus. We cannot do it with a cold indifferent experience, and as believers we are to be flames of fire. (Mark 16:17) And these signs shall follow them that believe; In my name shall they cast out devils; they shall speak with new tongues and shall take up serpents. We are called to be ministers of that resurrected life and power and healing virtue of Jesus Christ wherever we go.

Without Jesus, we can do nothing. Without His genuine anointing, our ministry is nothing but sounding brass and a tinkling cymbal. Every time we face a situation or in need, the Holy Ghost will bring that manifestation. We must understand that the Holy Spirit is omnipresent and he is everywhere, and it is the most marvelous thing for me to know that this Holy Ghost power can be in us all the time because we are His temple. You can feel it from the crown of your head to the soles of your feet every time you call on the name of Jesus and magnify that wonderful name. Oh, it is lovely to be burning all over with the Spirit of God! And when that takes place there is nothing but the operation of the gifts that brings forth the manifestation of His glory and the praise of His name.

AT THE WORKSHOP OF THE ENEMY

Raised and brought up by a religion that identifies with worshipping millions of gods from one generation to another generation, I was an apprentice to my grandmother who was into idol worshipping and witchcraft from the time I was ten years old. I served not only thousands but millions of gods, in fact to be specific around three hundred and thirty millions gods. I observe from the young age the powers of darkness working in the lives of these devotees as they gave their lives totally and unreserved to these gods. I personally watched how my grandma as a witch doctor will commune with these spirits and was endowed with powers to read of the past and predict the future of her followers. There will be a long line of people waiting in queue, waiting from dawn to dusk wanting to consult her for various needs and soothsaying. She will be under the trance of these spirits and would require them to do rituals to remove the curses that have afflicted them. As I return to bed at night I will be consumed with much fear and oppression by these spirits and I could hear their voices echoing in my ears. I would isolate from people and feel hopeless.

> *When God so loved the world He did not form a committee and wait for suggestions but came and laid himself on the cross for you and me as a ransom for Sin.*
>
> **Phil 2:8**

But thank God for the works of the cross and the power of the blood that break every power of hell and sets us free from every darkness (Revelation 12:11) *"And they overcame him (Satan) by the blood of the Lamb, and by the word of their testimony."*

Even today believers can undergo oppression of the enemy. There are many ways a believer can be oppressed;

1. Straying thoughts "that are not you."
2. Having sudden depression.
3. Having suicidal thoughts.
4. Having fits of anger or rage that are unusual.
5. Feeling hopeless and loss of direction.
6. Personality changes like fear or wanting to be isolated all the time.
7. Feelings that an area, like in your house, that there is something heavy, depressive or oppressive.

WHEN ALL HOPE WAS GONE

When I was seventeen years old my mother was diagnosed with 3rd stage cancer in her stomach and was given six months to live. We would go from one doctor to another, one medium to another and one god after the other but there was no help found. We were tired of running from place to place and we drained all our finances and resources in search of her healing in total desperation and lost all hope on the gods we served for generations. It was the lowest part of my life where I was counting the days that my mother will be gone from us forever. It was late one night when I was home alone,

Jesus is the Good Shepherd giving His life, seeking His lost sheep. Turn over the leaves of the Bible and you can track His footprints from Eden for long centuries.

suddenly I heard a knock at the door and as I reached the door and opened it there stood an old woman gazing into my eyes. As I stood there looking at her suddenly she said "Son you have tried everything, why don't you try Jesus now, He will not fail you." I tried to explain to her that I don't need this western religion believe but she was gone and I stood there with a last option Jesus. Later I realize it was an encounter from heaven. I fell to my knees and I said "Jesus if you're God please show me that you can heal my mother and lift us from this misery." That's all I said and when I opened my eyes there was a light that shine about the place I knelt and a great presence and peace flooded my heart. It was so peaceful that I didn't want to stand up from that place.

I went to bed that night with great peace and as I was half asleep there was a presence that entered my room and I heard an audible voice that said" I came looking for you because you called for me, I will heal your mother and bless your family, I'm Jesus who died for you." As the voice ended I rose from the bed to see who was talking to me and there was no one in my room and I could not return back to sleep and so I stayed awake till the morning after that encounter with the one that defeated death and rose to life eternal. *Jesus is the Good Shepherd giving His life, seeking His lost sheep. Turn over the leaves of the Bible and you can track His footprints from Eden to Eternity.*

I dashed out from my house to the churches nearby looking for this Jesus, I was not looking for a religion but I was looking for the One whose voice was the sweetest, his presence was like none other and in his words was life eternal. My search for Him took me from one church to another till I was led to an apostolic church which i believed walked in that fullness of that resurrection and power. At the place, the Holy Spirit descended and I felt overshadowed by Him and all my heavy sins rolled away as I entered His throne room, immersed in his presence for full three hours. This experienced changed my Destiny, I could not return to where I was after these encounters with Him.

Later I took my mother to their revival meetings as her days was getting closer to the dateline the doctors had given. As her last days on earth was approaching fast as by this time doctor had only given her weeks to be alive she took a leap of faith and came to a Christian gathering. On the third day as she was sitting at the back of the row fighting for her last heart beat on earth with much pain and agony, drowsed by drugs given by the physicians suddenly the visiting evangelist called her and said "Jesus want to heal your cancer."

> *The mocker and the scoffer may not like our— presentation of who Jesus is but what does one do with an empty wheelchair and crutches that are thrown down by a cripple?*

As she went forth anxiously not knowing what will take place she was prayed for at the altar and as the man of

God laid his hands on her she sensed like as of water that flows from her head and ran through to her feet. As the water flows into her she realizes that all the pain that was in her body that made her bend over in agony was leaving her and she had received a healing miracle. She was dancing and praising Jesus with such a joy, a woman that had served millions of gods but One touch of the master's hand has made her whole and now worshipping the Lamb seated on the throne.

From that day onward she needed no more drugs, no more medication and no more pain as the Physician of all physicians have done it again.

A TESTIMONY THAT STOOD THE TEST OF MAN

Two weeks later when we took her to the same doctors who have diagnosed her and said she has only a few weeks to live and given her a death warrant, now was totally astonished to see her miracle and demanded to know what has taken place and where has she been to as they could not find any traces of cancer.

As I sat across these most learned men of medicine they kept saying this is impossible, how can this happen. "I told them my doctor Jesus did it" and we left the hospital with a clean bill of any cancer on her. It was a day where the angels had joined with us celebrating and glorifying Jesus of this miracle that shook the very elect and the noble man of knowledge in believing there is a risen Christ that is alive and miracles are still happening because He is Alive. As we walked out of the hospital we knew beyond any ounce of doubt that this healing miracle has taken place in a mortal body through the hands of an immortal God.

As we walked out of that place we were like one of them in the crowd that followed Jesus as on the way He met another big group on the opposite direction but these crowd had death on their minds, the corpse of a young man and the whole town had turned out distressed for a mother who had lost her son, a widow weeping and wailing and demonstrating as only easterners can. But the crowd with Jesus had him, the resurrection and the Life who held the keys to life and death walking triumphantly alongside with Him.

This was the group of people that was jubilant and joyful because they have tasted his Love and mercy. Hundreds if not thousands had been at the door of sickness at the door of death, inflicted with infirmities and now they are healed and made whole. The deaf hearing, the blind see and the crippled dancing joyfully following Jesus for miles to Nain. As we walked past the other group from the opposite direction, one has no hope and future but grave and with a multitude that has tasted the newness of life, Joy and deliverance led by this Jesus and though we could hear his voice echoing as we walked out of the hospital. "I'm the resurrection and Life." "Whosoever believe in me will never die (Jn 11:26)" This was the dawn of a new journey with him, life of the resurrection and power of the cross. Everything that the prophets of old spoke of him came as a revelation walked on the face of this earth and to us now.

We must have the stamp of approval from the Lord, who was marred more than any man and when he touched human frailty, it will be reconstructed. He spoke as no man had spoken and touched lives as no prophets nor angels did, He is the initiator of a world redemption. He was full of compassion and made all things to move until the people said "We never saw anything like this" He was truly God that was manifested in the flesh redeeming the lost and the powerless out of his love and compassion. One touch of the master's hand is all we need to be made whole and well, redeemed just like the woman that came to him with the issue of blood for twelve years. Just one touch from the master, she didn't return to the life she had before, a testimony that stood in history before men and angels.

> *As the dew of the night refreshes the scorched grass so the dew of the love of Jesus refreshes the deep longing soul for him.*

Then the eyes of the blind will be opened, And the ears of the deaf will be unstopped. Then the lame will leap like a deer, and the tongue of the dumb will shout for joy. For waters will break forth in the wilderness and streams in the Arabah.
(*Isaiah 35:5-6*)

Rom 6;23 For the wages of sin is death; but the gift of God is eternal life through Jesus Christ our Lord.

2 YOU SHALL RECEIVE POWER

Acts 1:8
But ye shall receive power, after that the Holy Ghost is come upon you: and ye shall be witnesses unto me both in Jerusalem, and in all Judea, and in Samaria, and unto the uttermost part of the earth.

When John the Baptist introduced Jesus, he introduces him as a fire baptizer. John has been baptizing the multitudes unto repentance from dead works until Jesus showed up. In Matt 3:11 John says "I indeed baptize you with water unto repentance but He that is cometh after me whose shoes I'm not worthy to carry." He will baptize you with the Holy Spirit and with fire. The word baptized in Greek means to be dipped and immersed completely from head to toe. People normally identify this with the baptism of the water in immersion but how about when John said "Ye shall be baptized with the Holy spirit and with fire". The word baptism is also used in the commercial world, used in the trade of dyers. When the cloth is dipped completely into the dye, it is known as baptized. The cloth in the dye and the dye in the cloth. The cloth accepts the color, texture and the character of the dye. When Jesus baptize us with his spirit we are not only the recipient of his spirit but also we are immersed in his Spirit and Fire. We are in

> *When John introduced Jesus he introduced him as the Spirit and fire baptizer.*

the fire and the fire in us. We look, we appear and our new identity is of the fire of the Holy Ghost. There is no more place for carnality and dead works. We are to be hot like the one hundred and twenty in the upper room freshly filled with the baptism of the fire. We become partakers of the divine nature of Jesus, verse 7 and 8 says to be witnesses. When the Holy Spirit comes on us, it transforms us into a powerouse of witness, in other words we will find favor in the sight of God and man.

BLESSED ARE THOSE THAT HUNGER

When I was a new born again believer, I use to attend revival services frequently at our local city to pray for those that came seeking for the Holy Spirit. On one occasion there was a lady that came night after night seeking to be filled with the baptism of the Holy Spirit. On the final night, she told the Lord that she will not return back home unless she was filled with this experience. At previous times she has been to many churches and some told her in order to receive the spirit of God she need to roll on the floor, she rolled but nothing happen, she was told to jump and she jumped but nothing happen, she was told to run around the aisles and because of her hunger she did but she went back home empty and disappointed. When we met her at the church service she was ready for the Lord to fill her and I encourage her to simply worship Him. As she lifted both her hands toward heaven and worshipped Jesus with all her heart and soul, God filled her with a beautiful experience and she spoke in a beautiful heavenly language she did not learn before. Her face lit up as of thousands of light bulbs and the glory of God came upon her. Even though it was almost midnight and everybody has gone back home but God saw the hunger in her and visited her in the fullness of his glory.

When Moses came down from the mountain those that were with him had to put a veil on Moses' face as the glory of God was on him. When you are in the presence of the Almighty God and covered by his glory those that see you will know that you have been in the secret high place of the most glorious God.

There are reasons why some people struggle to receive the Holy Spirit

I. Doubt and Intellectual pride.

In the 1960, a journalist named John Sherrill decided to write a book desecrating the phenomenon of speaking in tongues. But after he interviewed a number of people about this experience his doubt shattered and he was baptized with the Holy Spirit himself. Later he wrote another book *'They speak with other tongues'* that became a Christian classic.

Spiritual experiences cannot be figured out with an intellectual mind. To receive the spirit infilling one must let go of the intellectual arguments and become as a child (Matt 18:2-4).

II. Emotional wounds

Some people are too burdened with emotional wounds to be filled with the Spirit. Some have been abused and hurt, others into depression and carry a spirit of grievance, they need to be healed first. As Lazarus been bound with grave clothes, some are bound with grave clothes of the past and they need to be unwrapped and delivered before they can experience God's infilling love and joy through his spirit.

> *A man with an experience is never at the mercy of a man with just an argument!*

III. Un-confessed Sins

God is holy (Is 43:15) and he cannot abode in a vessel that is not cleansed and ready for his holiness The vessel needs washing with the blood of the Lamb because God is holy and our hidden and un-confessed sin will prevent God from filling us with his presence. Repentance is not mere a confession from the mouth but redirection from the past life. Some people 'stuff' their secret sins in the closet of their hearts. If you want to be filled with the Holy Spirit you must be willing to open that closet and invite the light of God into every dark corner of your life. No surgeon can operate and give us a sinless heart. No therapist can rid us of selfishness or hate. Its Jesus and Jesus alone that is able to do this supernatural surgery.

IV. Religious tradition

I know a seventh-day Adventist preacher who had an encounter with some of his church folks that had brought a girl possessed with demons and they wanted this pastor to rebuke and cast these tormenting spirits out from this girl. As this preacher prayed and rebuked these spirits suddenly the girl began to laugh loudly, informing all his members and said "You have no power to cast us out because you're not a child of God" Ashamed, he withdrew himself and later some of his members told him about our church and invited him to visit us for a special service and seek after the Holy Spirit.

Initially, when he came he had a lot of struggles with his theologies, traditional teachings but the moment he made up his mind to put off all those past traditions and truly seek after the lord. God filled him with the baptism of the Holy Ghost within minutes and he spoke in a beautiful language as the glory of God filled him. Later he went back and cast out many of the tormenting spirits in that girl and his ministry took off in the power of the spirit of God.

THE AUTHORITY OF A BELIEVER

Binding and loosing. Matthew 18:18 relates to the church. Jesus is linking the church and authority he gave through the Spirit. When believers take the authority in the name of Jesus and He confirms it because his word says greater is he that is in us than he that is in the world. God has handed over authority to us when we became his children through the adoption of his spirit. Apostolic authority and the Gifts of the Spirit are given to those who live a life of prayer, fasting, and consecration to God.

When I was pastoring the first church, after some time the church people brought in a girl that was been possessed with many demonic spirits. They did not bring it to my attention at first and took it into their hands and began to pray for her at her home and every night the demon spirit would manifest very violently and even some of the people could not even hold her down as she will be strong as 7 strong men. Finally, after few days battling with these demons, they informed me and we went with two intercessors to pray for her. The moment this girl saw us it turn against us with high pitch voice and said 'You can't cast us out' I said yes I can't cast you out but Jesus Can. Within the next hour, hundreds of demons were leaving her body as we commanded them to go in the name of Jesus. In Jesus name, it has to obey and submit!

> *Apostolic authority and the Gifts of the Spirit are given to those who live a life of prayer, fasting, and consecration to God.*

Jesus was not a martyred victim, but a mighty victor, he took upon himself the form of a man to hunt and destroy the enemy and his power. God overthrew our greatest enemy, sin, and our final foe, death. The world ran true to form when it crucified him. He turned red blood into royal redemption. Men took a lovely tree, stripped it, and twisted it into the stark beams of the cross. It was their logo of hate. Jesus picked it up, stained it with His life's blood, and gave it back to us—His logo was love and victory.

The early chapters of the book of Acts tell us that the disciples together with 120 were filled with the Holy Spirit and there were seen cloven tongues of fire which sat on them as they spoke in tongues and magnified God. The rest of the book reads that they went on being filled from moment to moment to an overflowing life of the spirit. Living in the spirit is Power-Christianity not plastic, static institution. It is like a tree bursting with life and life abundantly.

In Heb 6:1-2 says "Therefore leaving the principles of the doctrine of Christ, let us go on unto perfection; not laying again the foundation of repentance from dead works, and of faith toward God." When someone is constantly struggling with issues of his flesh, carnal affections and constantly battling with weakness in his flesh without having experienced the true divine deliverance by the blood of Jesus. one will not understand what is it to have a resurrection power walking in the spirit not in accordance with the flesh.

God has brought us to a new order of things, a life of victory and overcoming beyond every comprehension of human mind. This overcoming state will only be embraced through walking in the spirit constantly. A person who has been fully saturated with the presence of the spirit will clearly understand his mission in the kingdom of God. When the Holy Spirit possesses a person with all his fullness his whole being will be saturated with the power from high. We are transformed to sons and daughters of God and the habitation of the God who is all light, all revelation, all power, all truth and all love. To have more of the Holy Spirit is to have more of that agape love, (Rom 5:5).

> *When the Holy Spirit possesses a person with all his fullness our whole being will be saturated with His power from high*

AN EXPERIENCE THAT CHANGE ME FOREVER

How joyful I was when God filled me with the baptism of the Holy Spirit shortly after my mother's healing. When I first heard of the Holy Spirit, the need to seek him for redemption and to be born again (Matt3:1-3) I went seeking, fasting, knocking on heaven's door. Night after night I would tarry in long prayers knocking on the heaven's door asking him to give me this infilling of his spirit.

Then on one occasion when I attended a local conference in a certain city, I witnessed how God began filling all those hungry souls that came seeking for the Holy Ghost. On the third night I was at the altar seeking him and worshipping with all my heart suddenly God began to flood my soul with his spirit as the spirit gave the utterance, i spoke in a heavenly language and magnified him for a full hour.

After everybody left the conference hall God began to move me aside and as I was in his presence, I was filled again and the heavenly cloud overshadowed me for full three hours. In the next morning when I rose up from the bed preparing for the morning devotion again God visited me and flooded my soul with his beautiful presence. It was a heavenly experience, I don't want anything but to be in that state forever.

When I returned home from that meeting for a full week I forgot about going to school, fellowshipping with others, eating. I was in a different realm; the realm of God. It was so glorious, so wonderful as I felt like Moses felt on the mountain separated from everyone and saturated with the presence and the glory of God. I just long to be in that secret place. My family saw the difference, my friends saw the difference and those that were close to me noticed that something powerful has taken hold of me. It is something wonderful, remarkable, so divine and so powerful beyond word can describe and out of this world.

May there be within us a deep hunger and thirst with a penetration that is centered entirely upon the axle of Him. To experience a deeper dimension of God's presence, your soul must hunger and thirst for God in the same way, a deer pants for the safety and sustenance of water. Only a small percentage of believers ever really experience this kind of intimacy with God because of the great price.

> *Living in the spirit is Power-Christianity not plastic, static institution. It is like a tree bursting with life and life abundantly.*

Psalm 42:1-2 declares, "As the hart [male red deer] panteth after the water brooks, so panteth my soul after thee, O God. My soul thirsteth for God, for the living God: when shall I come and appear before God?"

In the natural, the panting of the deer is an audible agonizing for the safety of the waters provided when pursued by a predator. When the deer runs into the water, the predator can no longer detect its scent. In addition to finding safety from its enemies, the deer finds relief from thirst in the waters. This is a place, our hiding place in God -- the place so safe and secure from every attack and circumstance where He keeps me safe in Him filling my souls with his living waters. There, *"under the shadow of the Almighty,"* I am safe from stalking enemies.

"Intimacy with God is found only in the realm of the spirit of God." Spiritually, your process of discovering a deeper dimension of God's presence involves longing, thirsting, seeking and waiting on him. David wrote, *"O God, thou art my God; early will I seek thee: my soul thirsteth for thee, my flesh longeth for thee in a dry and thirsty land, where no water is; to see thy power and thy glory, so as I have seen thee in the sanctuary"* (Psalm 63:1-2). Intimacy with God is found only in the realm of the spirit of God. There is a place of deep anointing, deep presence, and deep intimacy with God Almighty where "deep calleth unto deep" or spirit calls unto spirit. 'Deep calleth unto deep at the noise of thy waterspouts: all thy waves and thy billows are gone over me'.

It is a place that is so pure that every part of your being is consumed by the presence of Almighty God; a deep place where there is perfect communion between your spirit and every dimension of God's presence.

Your soul is stirred and there is a breakthrough in the spirit as "deep calleth unto deep" (Psalm 42:7).

God plans for nothing to be ordinary. Jesus pointed to the lilies as examples of superb beauty, every petal and leaf perfection. In the Kingdom of God, the extraordinary is so common, it is just ordinary.

Ps 42:1-2 As the hart panteth after the water brooks, so panteth my soul after thee, O God. My soul thirsteth for God, for the living God: when shall I come and appear before God?

3 STEPPING INTO THE MIRACULOUS

John 14:12-14
Verily, verily, I say unto you, He that believeth on me, the works that I do shall he do also; and greater works than these shall he do; because I go unto my Father. And whatsoever ye shall ask in my name, that will I do, that the Father may be glorified in the Son.

When I was converted to my new found faith those that were close to me and my relatives from my previous religious believe, became estranged. At that time they could not comprehend and understand the love relation I had embraced with my Jesus. During those early years people tried to bring many persecutions against us, at times I felt like an insignificance candle in a great world. But the darker the world is, the brighter the light of the spirit shined. John 1:5 says *'And the light shineth in darkness; and the darkness comprehended it not'*.

The darkness neither can understand the light nor has it the power to quench the light. The glow of the light will lit up in every place it is put forth. Many times believers would ask me what it takes to make a Christian live exciting and I will always tell them that the life in the spirit and the fellowship with the resurrected Lord brings the joy and is always exciting. When there is a deep relationship with him and he walks with us and talks with us, every day is a new day, every moment is like a fresh breath.

As the dew of night refreshes the sun-scorched grass and the lilies that grow in the valley, so the dew of the presence of God refreshes the longing within us for Him. We grow into the thing that fills our thoughts, as inevitably as the stream merges into the ocean.

FIRE FROM HEAVEN

The bible declares that God is a consuming fire (Heb12:29) and that fire often appears as a symbol of God's presence. When Moses appeared before the burning bush (Exodus 3:2), the shekinah glory (Exodus 14:19, Numb 9:15-16) from that fire radiates the light and the power of God and it will pierce every darkness and the work of the enemies. Fire is a wonderful image of the Holy Spirit. The Spirit of God is like a fire in three different dimensions:

> *His first disciples followed Him just when He signaled. It was just Him, not what He did for them, no money, no honor, no splendor and no place to lay their head.*

i) **It is the presence of the Almighty God**

Though the earth is full of God's presence, many could not perceive it. God made a covenant with his people in the old testament church desiring them to be a kingdom of priests and holy nation (Exo 19 6). He made his presence visible to them by manifesting himself in fire, smoke and in a cloud and speaking to them through thunder, fire and lightning.

In Acts chapter 2 when the disciples received this same presence inside of them, they were transformed. It was the same fire and glory now shut in earthen vessels. They no longer need to look for the outer manifestation presence as the same glorious presence is within them and us now. It is the very reason why the bible *says* **'Know ye not that ye are the temple of the Holy Spirit' (1Cor3:16).**

ii) **The Spirit of God brings a passion for God.**

The Holy Spirit creates the passion for Him in our hearts. On the road to Emmaus, the two travellling disciples communed with the resurrected Jesus and describe that their hearts "burning within us' (Luke 24:32)

After the apostles receiving the infilling of the Holy Spirit on the day of Pentecost, Peter stood up and spoke with passion and boldness (Acts 2:14-42). It was not only the voice of God heard on that day but this same disciple who denied Jesus previously couple of weeks earlier for fear of losing his life now standing in the midst of the same group proclaiming this resurrected Jesus as the messiah that saw three thousand people. The bible says those who believed what Peter said were baptized. And added to the church that day—about 3,000 in all. They had a passion that lasted for a life time and impels them to speak the word of God boldly (Acts 4:31).

I pray that believers will not grow old in our first love, the experience we had with the Lord and with the spirit of God. I believe everyone of us had a remarkable experience with the Lord on our conversion, when we were filled fresh with that baptism of the Spirit we are filled with zeal and passion and some of us even went beyond and made many vows at one time. We want to reach out to as many and witness about the new life in Jesus and speak of his love. We should always stay in his presence and be filled over and over with his spirit to carry the passion during our lifetime. Our passion will continue to live and burn as long as we have a deep hunger, positioning ourselves to be overshadowed by his glory over and over again in that secret place. As sinners, we hated what God loves and loved what God hated but When we were born-again and found life in the spirit we begin to love what God loves and hate what God hates.

When I received the baptism of his spirit, I spread the gospel like a wild fire. I want to tell and witness to everyone that I met about Jesus. At one time I was witnessing to the group of students from the Hindu groupsin my high school. They were very furious to find out whyI betrayed my Hindu beliefs and embraced Christianity and they took council and brought in the authorities to put me in some problems. They plotted to expel me from theschool but when they could not do anything against me these groups brought in the news press and published in the papers that if anyone is caught preaching in school they will be expelled. Nevertheless many that heard my testimony came to the Lord. God gave a divine love and passion for these people.

iii) **The Spirit of God brings the purity and holiness of God in our lives.**

God purpose is to purify us (Titus 2:14 *Who gave himself for us, that he might redeem us from all iniquity, and purify unto himself, a peculiar people, zealous of good works*) and He is a refining fire(Mal 3:3 *And he shall sit as a refiner and purifier of silver and he shall purify the sons of Levi, and purge them as gold silver, that they may offer unto the Lord an offering in righteousness*) and the spirit of God is an ambassador of our sanctification 1Cor 6:11- And *such were some of you: but ye are washed, but ye are sanctified, but ye are justified in the name of the Lord Jesus, and by the Spirit of our God.*

> *As sinners we hated what God loves and loved what God hated but when we were born again we begin to love what God love and hate what God hates.*

As the silversmith uses fire to purge the dross from the precious metal so God uses His spirit to remove all sins, impurities, unrighteousness from us.(Psalms 66:10). His fire cleanses and refines.

2 Cor 5:1-4: *For we know that if our earthly house of this tabernacle were dissolved, we have a building of God, a house not made with hands, eternal in the heavens. For in this we groan, earnestly desiring to be clothed upon with our house which is from heaven If so be that being clothed we shall not be found naked. For we that are in this tabernacle do groan, being burdened: not for that we would be unclothed, but clothed upon, that mortality might be swallowed up of life.*

Moses armed with a shepherd's rod fought against the greatest military power on earth. Moses said "Who am I?" but God said "I am who I am". (Exodus 3:11, 4:14.) Who He is with him - that is what matters, not who Moses was, nor who we are. It is 'Christ in us the hope of glory". Where Moses walked he left the footmarks of God and the Spirit of God has left a footmark in all of us since the day of Pentecost.

When I gave my heart to the Lord and had the beautiful experience of his visitation, brought under his overshadowing glory of the spirit it was more than I can ask for. It was an experience that changed my course and my destiny. I want to tell to everyone, every person that come along my way about the man of Galilee that transformed my life.

> *"We are partakers of the Divine nature" (2 Peter 1:4), directed by the living river the world knows nothing about. "As many as are led by the Spirit of God THEY are the children of God"—and that is our distinctive mark in the world!*

When we live in the river of God, totally immersed in his love, healing is released through us. Rich life springs up along the banks of our lives. This living water from God not only transforms us but to all those we may come in contact with. It makes bitter water to taste sweet. His love flows through as a result of the intimate love found in the secret place. We have to enter into this life giving river in order to experience and carry its pure water in our souls to others. One we are immersed in His River we will not only know Him in the power of the resurrection and the fellowship of his suffering but carry this living experience wherever we go even to the darkest places.

AN OPEN DOOR FOR A MIRACLE.

Some people come to Him with a small little idea and perception of his fullness and many are satisfied with a thimbleful and dab. The word declares that to him that believeth nothing is impossible - all things are possible through the seed of faith (Mark 9:23).

The Gifts of the Spirit are not medals of Honor to be worn on Sunday morning at church. They are tools for the job in the kingdom and are dished out when you report for God's work. He won't give you a hammer when you need a power chainsaw. The Lord will give you any miracle-tool you need that moment - either to heal the sick or to raise the dead. This is my experience.

If we only could hear the voice of God saying "Oh if they only knew how much they could receive "if they knew to come to my 'secret place'.

On one occasion as a new believer, I went to visit some friends, as I was talking to them in their living room all of a sudden I heard a loud scream coming from the back of the house and again after few minutes, I heard the same scream again. I inquired of the family who is this person and why is he screaming, first there was silence and then the daughter broke the silence sobbing and told me that her father is dying and he is in great pain. They told me he was diagnosed with ulcer in his stomach, they brought him to the hospital and the doctors kept him for six months and when the ulcer has turned into cancer and the doctors had given up hope on him and told them to take him back home. Because of the severity of the pain he would scream throughout the day and night and wanted to kill himself, many times they tried to stop him, he is about 70 years old.

As I sat there I heard the sweet voice of my Jesus telling me 'Go in and see this man, I asked them if I could see this man. They took me to the back of the house where there was a small room and as I open the door of the room a foul smell merge out from that room, it stink so badly and I went into that dark room anyway. As they switch on the light I saw an old frail figure of a dying man at the corner of the room. He was probably has not washed or taken his bath for over six months. The moment he saw me, he tried

> *The gifts of the spirit are not Medal of Honor to be worn on Sunday morning at the church. They are tools for the job in the kingdom and are dished out when you report to the Master and for His task*

to stand up and said "Son please bring me a knife I don't want to live anymore, I can't bear this pain"

As I stood in that cold I felt the warmth love of Jesus filling that room, it was wonderful when the master walks into any situation, every gloom, darkness and death will flee in his presence. Suddenly I was not aware of the bad odor in that place nor the people that were resent in that room. All I heard was "Love him with my love."

I quickly asked the daughter to make a bowl of porridge and fed him since he has not eaten for 4 days and sat him back on his bed. Before I left that place I said 'Jesus I did what I could do now you need to do what you can do for this dying man and I left that home. After two weeks I returned back to that home and have forgotten everything about that man. There were no more noise, no more screaming and it was silent at that house. As we were sitting and talking in the living room I heard someone coming down from upstairs walking down the stairs.

When I turned to look this was the same dying old man at the back of the house, unable to walk and now came walking with a big smile on his face. He came to me and said 'Thank you son, your Jesus healed me. I'm completely healed without any more pain and cancer. Their family burst into tears of Joy and what a day it was when salvation visited their home that day.

We must have the stamp of our loving Lord, who was marred more than any other man.

And when He touched human weakness, it will be reconstructed. He spoke out of the depth of trial and mockery and became the redeemer of the world. The man never spoke as he spoke. He was full of love and compassion made all things to move until the people said "We never saw anything like this." He was truly God manifested in the flesh in power and glory. He can take the weak and make them strong.

It can be debated that this or that religion is better than another, but the Gospel offers only one thing—JESUS. He is the only One opening his arms to all people. Blessed are they that hunger and thirst for Him, for they shall be filled. He is everything. He is the Alpha and Omega. The Lord said, "He who believes in me has everlasting life" (Jn 6:47). Jesus is not a religion. He is a Person to meet and live by, the living Word walked and clothed in flesh and blood. He is not a messenger from God. He is the living Message of life and life abundantly that come through the living word. *But he was wounded for our transgressions, he was bruised for our iniquities: the chastisement of our peace was upon him; and with his stripes we are healed (Is 53:5).*

Jesus always taught the people and then demonstrated his authority as God by his miracles. It is astounding that the religious groups accepted the miracles but denied his ability to forgive sins. Today it's just the opposite, many people have no problem to believe for the forgiveness of sins and even for the infilling of the Holy Spirit but absolutely resistance to the idea that Jesus wants to heal everyone.

The bible clearly shows that Jesus healed those that needed healing through his word, through faith and through his compassion.

Every time faith and compassion is present we can see the supernatural demonstration of healings and miracles taking place. Mark 16:20 describes the first disciples of Jesus "They went forth everywhere and the Lord working with them." God's presence is unconditional. This great truth is not put together from isolated texts but is woven into the texture of the whole revelation of God.

THE SUPERNATURAL REALM

Understanding this some ask the question and the controversy that surfs around ministries and man of God that manifest the healing and the supernatural demonstration;

  I. Does God heal everyone?
  II. Whose faith is necessary, the sick person or the minister?

III. Why are some people not healed?

God works in the supernatural realm through many aspects which include;

1) Through the Gift of Healing.

1 Cor 12:9 - To another faith by the same Spirit; to another the gifts of healing by the same Spirit.

There are times when God releases the gift of healing in a certain places, in a revival or healing crusade meetings.

When these gifts are in operation the evidence of the supernatural is so visible and undeniable. Sometime these gifts are accompanied by the word of faith and the word of authority over the demonic influences and the physical bodies. Once this yoke of infirmity has been broken the people will experience the flooding of God's healing river flowing into them.

> *Jesus is not a religion, He is a person to meet and live by, the living word that walked and clothed in flesh and blood. He is not a messenger from God but rather the living message.*

When I was in Bangladesh at a hill side place at one time the believers took me to revival gathering where I was supposed to speak to over seven hundred Muslims in an auditorium and to pray for the sick. When we got there so many people already gathered an hour before and I was surrounded with so many people from the Muslim background. We were the only Christian in the midst of these crowd that turned up to see if Jesus is alive as they were told. We had people on crutches, wheelchairs, cripple, blind, deaf and mute. When I saw them I was overwhelmed by their hunger for Jesus. Their Holy book says that Jesus is the only prophet that can heal and set free an inflicted soul. Even before we could finish speaking, the crowd came rushing to the altar with their infirmities and diseases. As we lifted our hands and prayed that

Jesus would heal and set these people free from their bondage, it was like a blanket of fog that fell on the people

The chains of bondages were being broken in front of our eyes as the cloud of God's glory covered these people, we heard the people screaming when the power of God hit them, then one by one they left the crutches and the wheelchairs behind and started to walk up to the stage to testify of the glorious touch of the Lord and to be prayed for. There was a long line on both sides as the people were excited to give a testimony and wanted to be prayed for. Healing miracles began to flood the congregation and almost everyone was healed and the end result was they wanted Jesus.

Psalms 107:13-14 "Then they cried unto the Lord in their trouble, and he saved them out of their distresses, He brought them out of darkness and the shadow of death, and brake their chains in sunder."

When Jesus shows up in any place, anything can happen especially the supernatural manifestation and lives transformed under the power of the Holy Spirit.

People are told that the preaching of the Gospel is "past its sell-by date." But while some are still muttering their unbelief, He is working innumerable healings, signs, wonders and miracles in our present days when his name is mentioned.

He comes walking on the roaring sea of pain, disease and infirmity, offering himself as the fountain of life and salvation. Never in history has it been so evident that Jesus is alive and well, risen from the dead, working among us as He worked in the days of His flesh. Where ever there is a sinner that seeks him with his whole being, He comes to the scene as he did in the days of old.

Matt 4:23 *And Jesus went about all Galilee, teaching in their synagogues, and preaching the gospel of the kingdom, and healing all manner of sickness and all manner of disease among the people.*

2) Through the laying of Hands

It is a privilege of every true believer to lay hands on the sick and pray for their healings. When someone places his hand there is a spiritual transference that takes place in the invisible realm. *Mark 16:18-They shall take up serpents; and if they drink any deadly thing, it shall not hurt them; they shall lay hands on the sick, and they shall recover.*

First, the person laying on hands may thereby transmit spiritual blessing, authority or anointing to the one upon whom hands are laid; second, the person laying on hands may thereby acknowledge publicly some spiritual blessing or authority already received from God by the one upon whom hands are laid; third, the person laying on hands may thereby publicly commit to God for some special task or ministry the one upon whom hands are laid. At times, all these three purposes may be combined in one and the same act of laying on hands.

Many times people have told me that when they see me laying hands on the people they see another hand on those prayed for, this must be the hand of the Lord because I'm not the one that is able to heal and set them free, it's Jesus and always has been the Master.

> *People are told that the preaching of the gospel is past its sells-by date. But while there are some that are still muttering their unbelief, He is working innumerable healings, signs wonders and miracles in our present days*

The laying on of hands is a channel through which the supernatural gift of healings operates. In such a case, the person who lays on hands by this act transmits the supernatural healing virtue, or power, of God to the body of the one on whom hands are laid; and very often this latter person actually feels within his own body the supernatural power of God.

One time during a revival services in Malaysia we had some great move of God in our midst and God was present to heal and set the people free. After the service on the second night, some Chinese people approached me and said if I could go to a caregiver place to pray for their sister as she was longing to come for the service but she is not able to come because she was paralyzed. The next morning we took some believers and the family with us to that place where she was been taken care of and as we approached her, her faith was high for a miracle touch from the Lord and she said 'I have waited for this moment for 3 years' We laid our hands on her and she collapsed to the floor, as she woke up she stood on her feet and said she feel strange tingling all over her feet and her back and experiencing heat senses going through her body the next moment we saw she was walking on her own and without any aid. The next morning she packed her bags and went back home.

3) Through the Healing Anointing.

When the glory of God descends in certain places, you can know that his glorious anointing is there for a purpose. The birth of the church in the book of acts was announced by a rushing mighty wind (Acts 2:20) a tornado from heaven and later accompanied by the anointing fire that sat upon the one hundred and twenty.

> *We can walk into the devil's territory and rearrange his borders through the Anointing.*

There is a great danger when some churches that are born by this supernatural manifestation no longer hold on to the work and manifestation of the spirit due to their desire to become respectable decorous and conforming to the pattern of mega churches, the anointing and supernatural is ruled out of their meetings. Pentecost came with a mighty rushing wind and with fire and it did not stop there, there was a repetition in Acts 4 when the apostles prayed for boldness after they were threatened not to speak in the name of Jesus.

The Anointing of the Spirit fell in the place they gathered and it shook the place, the apostles did not run away seeing the manifestation of the spirit but they stayed under the covering of the Spirit until all of them were endowed with boldness and power from high. No wonder later as Peter walked on the streets of Jerusalem the people brought those that were sick and laid them on the streets as his shadow touched these sick people they were raised from their bed and a mighty revival swept through the city.

We need to stay in the place of the presence of the Lord and be covered again and again with this glorious anointing if we want to become mighty witnesses for Him. Many times when I'm in a meeting under the glorious presence of Jesus, I felt my flesh would be ripped apart because of the heaviness of the anointing, but this is not something that we need to be afraid of. When the anointing is present the manifestation of the supernatural is evident. It's like you're overshadowed under his glory and when its gets thicken it will saturate you with its fullness until it overflows from you to other people. Everyone that come in contact with the anointing will be set free.

I was at one time in India for their conference and while we worshipped the mighty anointing fell and hit the people. It was like waves and waves of water that flowed in, we need not to lay hands on anyone. Many fell to the ground prostrate when this anointing hits, speaking in tongues. The presence and the power of God was present to fill them with His spirit and heal them all. The people were overshadowed under this anointing, nobody was lacking anything, nobody wants to go home, it was late at night passed the midnight hour. The musicians could not worship as usual, there were no ministering of man but the anointing of God has come in to minister to his people and they all were healed, delivered and filled with the mighty presence of the Spirit. It was glorious!

When our churches lack this presence and anointing, services will turn dull and stale, we will set time limits to the gathering and everything falls under programs and schedule where the spirit is not given liberty to have his way. Nothing moves in that place, everything is dead and silent.

The anointing of the Holy Spirit is given through people to demonstrate God's love and power. Christ means the "Anointed One". Because Christ is in us, the same anointing that He had on earth now belong to us. *(Luke 4:18-19 NKJV) "The Spirit of the LORD is upon me, because He has anointed me to preach the Gospel to the poor; He has sent me to heal the brokenhearted, to proclaim liberty to the captives and recovery of sight to the blind, To set at liberty those who are oppressed; {19} To proclaim the acceptable year of the LORD."*

I will not return to such a place where the works of the flesh are present instead of the work of the spirit; where the people are full of traditions and Christian customs instead of the true love and hunger for Jesus and programs take over God. We can turn into spiritual antiques or we can be like the woman that came to Jesus with the issue of blood.

4) Through the spoken word of Rhema.

It is a spoken word of faith that will not return back void. Every time when the word of authority is spoken through faith, it sees the supernatural taking place.

Mark 11:23 For verily I say unto you, That whosoever shall say unto this mountain, Be thou removed, and be thou cast into the sea; and shall not doubt in his heart, but shall believe that those things which he saith shall come to pass; he shall have whatsoever he saith.

There are three foundation stones of faith that get results:

(1) Have faith in God [vs. 22] — faith in His Word and in the promises of God. It's not "faith in faith" or in memorized formulas that get results, but faith in God.
(2) Believe in your heart, without doubting.
(3) And say with your mouth what you believe.

What is a Rhema? Rhema is a spoken word for the moment, for NOW, for a specific situation that you are in now. Have you ever asked God to speak to you? And suddenly the preaching is about what you asked God to speak to you about? That is a Rhema.

Jesus did not walk the earth confessing promises; He walked with revealed faith. There has to be a place in the process of your walk with God that He has to speak with you supernaturally. The prophets come with Rhema words. A prophetic word gives direction.

One Rhema word is enough to change your destiny.

Believing God and His Word is of great importance. But Jesus encourages us further to articulate, to say aloud, what we are believing God for. There is great power in the spoken Rhema word.

> *God's ministers are to be a flame of fire—a perpetual flame, a constant fire, a continual burning, burning and shining the light of the spirit.*

Faith is an inward operation of the divine power that dwells in the contrite heart and can lay hold of the thing that are not seen.

Some time ago a Buddhist woman in Nepal was found to have cancer. Some faithful Christian brothers visited her and gave her the bible that we took to Nepal and read the passage from Psalms 107:20 *"He sent His word and healed them, And delivered them from their destructions."* She began to declare every day that God had sent His word to heal her. Day after day her health improved and she was completely healed went on to have a long life and later a church was founded in that area because of her testimony. The spoken word of faith applied the awesome power of God's Word to the woman's sick body, with spectacular results

4) Through the Realm of faith.

Understanding the realms of authority will also enhance and accent your God-given gifts. Many people try to operate in the spirit and do not understand spiritual realms. In order to understand spiritual realms, we must understand realms of authority. Though there are many kinds of authority, spiritual authority is the highest. If our authority in Christ is by the Spirit, it cannot relate to whether or not a person is a male or female, Jew or Gentile. There is no distinction between them in the spirit. The things of the spirit realm are very real, but they cannot be socially, scientifically or intellectually confirmed. The things of the spirit can only be spiritually discerned. Faith does not operates in the realm of possible, there is no glory for God in that which is humanly possible.

"Then Jesus told him, "Because you have seen me, you have believed; blessed are those who have not seen and yet have believed." -John 20:29.

This is the lowest realm of faith because you believe only because you see. Jesus demonstrated then he taught. Today, 95% of the churches preachers teach more than the demonstration of the work of the spirit. Teaching and preaching are important but it should not replace the work and the ministering of God's spirit to the needy. Many times those that come with a need in their life goes back empty because we have not allowed the ministry of the Spirit of God to take over to meet the needs of those that came. Churches have tight programmes on Sunday morning that God has to ask us the permission to come in to heal, restore, fill and bless his people.

Paul said—*"And my speech and my preaching was not with enticing words of man's wisdom, but in demonstration of the Spirit and of power"1 Cor 2:4*

In some meetings, until people see the realm of faith, the blind eyes seeing, the deaf ears opening, the lame walking and the dead are raised, they will not be ready to step in and receive for themselves a touch of miracle. When the first miracle takes place in any meeting it will be the forerunner to build faith for others to believe that it can happen to them too. When people have reached a level of faith, God is ready on the other end with a touch of supernatural, there will be chains of miracles taking place after the first one. People will now be able to see and believe that God is working at the scene, every testimony will be a building block of faith for another miracle to take place. When this hit in any meeting there will be rows and rows of testimony waiting to be heard and to glorify Jesus.

5) Through the name of Jesus.

Acts 3:1-8 - Then Peter said, Silver and gold have I none; but such as I have give I thee: In the name of Jesus Christ of Nazareth rise up and walk.

When you begin to speak the name of Jesus to every adversary and infirmity, the authority behind that name breaks every stronghold and chain upon the people and set the captives free. It is the only name that has the power to release deliverance and healing. The name of Jesus on the lips of ordinary men and women brings forth mighty works.

> *Faith does not operate in the realm of possible, there is no glory for God in that which is humanly possible.*

When we take on the name of Jesus, we are not just "believers." We are re-positioned as the apostles; it is a spiritual shift. We are no longer, standing up to be counted for Jesus as the ordinary but we are placed INSIDE of what His name represents. We live in Him, inside of us He lives. When the name of Jesus Christ is invoked, it carries all of the power, authority and distinction God gave to it. He raised from the dead, elevated to the position of power and authority, and the name of Jesus a *"Name above "every name that is named, not only in this age but also in that which is to come."* (Ephesians 1:21)

At one time when I was in India some believers had organized an evangelistic meeting in a certain village, since this village had never heard the gospel and the saving name of Jesus we were there for three nights. On the second night many people came to hear the good news of Jesus for the first time as all of them were Hindus.

There was one particular woman that was sitting under a coconut tree and listening to the word and while she was there about seven coconuts fell on her head and crushed her head. Her skull was broken and she was carried to the hospital by her relatives. The believers followed her to the hospital and in the surgery room they began to call on the name of Jesus, all the sudden that woman opened her eyes and said she wants to go back home. The doctors that was treating her was astonished at this miracle and she went back home well. When she got back to the village many people who saw and heard of this miracle began to turn to Jesus, when we touched to feel her skull there was no skull on top of her head, it's like a soft jelly and she is a walking miracle to this date filled with his spirit and Glory.

> *When we take on the name of Jesus, we are just not 'believers' we are re-positioned as the apostles was. It is a spiritual shift.*

Through the name of Jesus she defeated death because that name represent Jesus who defeated death and rose back again.

He is the resurrection and Life!

Acts 4:30 - By stretching forth thine hand to heal; and that signs and wonders may be done by the name of thy holy child Jesus.

4 THEN CAME THE GLORY

In the Kingdom of God, there are divine orders, there is difference between the natural and the spiritual, the outer court, inner court and the Holies of Holies. When we look at the outer court there is no beauty in that place, there is no covering, a place with a smell of blood and the frenzy of the dying creatures and the endless buckets of blood thrown on the altar. The shofar would sound and the men would wrest the lambs to the ground, slitting their throats.

As they bled to death, the priests standing next to them would catch the blood in large buckets. When these were full they would be passed up the line to those who stood by the altar. They would throw the blood against the side of the altar. The empty buckets would be recycled and refilled with the blood of more lambs. It is not a beautiful sight to look at the outer court. The sacrifice was offered upon the altar. Physically the priests passed the altar first before washing at the laver. To enter the Holy of Holies, the priests had to first pass through the gate of the outer court which was on the east toward the sunrise. Then they passed through the outer court into the Holy Place and then finally into the Holiest Place.

Without the sacrifice and the washing, the priest could not enter into the Holy Place to minister. The Holy Place has a covering over it and is illuminated by the radiance of the light from the golden candlestick. In the Holy place (inner court) of the tabernacle, the priest who served in the tabernacle received their light from the Menorah. Because of the animal skin which was used to cover the whole tabernacle, there was a very thick darkness which could not allow the priest to see what they were doing without light.

In Leviticus 24:1-3 God commanded the children of Israel through Moses to bring pure pressed olive oil, for the priest to use in the lighting of the menorah (seven branch lamp stand), so that the priest may be able to see what he was doing as he ministered on behalf of the congregation of Israel in the tabernacle of God. There is the Shew bread table with twelve Loaves of bread which represent the twelve tribes of Israel and The Altar of Incense.

THE SECRET PLACE FOR THE ANOINTING.

The Holy of Holies was constructed as a perfect cube. It contained only the Ark of the Covenant, the symbol of Israel's special relationship with God. The Holy of Holies was accessible only to the high priest. Once a year, on Yom Kippur, the Day of Atonement, the high priest was allowed to enter the small, windowless enclosure to burn incense and sprinkle the blood of a sacrificial animal on the mercy seat of the Ark. By doing so, the high priest atoned for his own sins and those of the people. The moment the sacrificial blood of the lamb is sprinkled between the two cherubim's at mercy seat, all of as sudden something remarkable would take place. The congregation on the outside of the court would hear the thunder, the lightning and see a cloud of God resting on the tabernacle.

> *We decide our eternal destiny, either to die in our sins or to die in Christ and be washed by His redeeming blood, to either end with a crown or a Coffin.*

When the glory of the Lord came down and filled the tabernacle for the first time it must have been an awesome spectacle to behold. God was truly pleased with His people, not because of their goodness but because their sins were covered and they were hid in Christ.

The high priest would have sensed a sweetness and the glorious manifestation when he encountered the Presence of the Lord in the holy of holies. The etymology of the dwelling or presence of God is the Hebrew word **Sh'cheenah** or as we pronounce it Shekinah. It is the majestic presence or manifestation of God in which He descends to dwell among men.

Whenever the invisible God becomes visible, and whenever the omnipresence of God comes with his fullest glory and power, this is the Shekinah Glory. But inside the Holy of Holies, something awesome will take place, as the glory of God sets in, the High priest will fall on his face to the ground and wait on the Glory in utmost fear and reverence. It doesn't matter how long it takes, as long the glory remains in that place the priest will remain prostrate on his face before the Lord.

Just like the High priest that entered the glory place; the Shekinah, God wants us to dwell in his presence because in His presence there is the fullness of Joy and at his right hand there are pleasures evermore. Once you have been to that secret place of the most high there is no place better on this earth. We must realize that developing a habit of dwelling in the presence of God continually is the only way to fulfill God-given destiny In us. This the key to a release of rivers of Anointing into our lives, his presence will draw us to the next level which is the glory and in the glory where the abundance of the anointing dwells.

Do you want to fulfill your divine destiny? You need the power of His presence.

We can have God's abiding presence and the innumerable power, it can lead. Meditate carefully and pray the prayer of Moses that accompanied it with holy aggression. 'If your presence doesn't go with me' Expect great results!

Exodus 33:13-15: *Now therefore, I pray thee, if I have found grace in thy sight, shew me now thy way, that I may know thee, that I may find grace in thy sight: and consider that this nation is thy people.*

[14] And he said, My presence shall go with thee, and I will give thee rest. [15] And he said unto him, If thy presence go not with me, carry us not up hence.

ENROLLING IN THE SCHOOL OF THE SPIRIT.

Moses knew it was God's presence in Israel that set the people apart from all other nations. And the same is true of the church of Jesus today. The only thing that sets us apart from ordinary believers is God's being "with us" - leading us, guiding us, working through his spirit in and through us.

Moses didn't care how other nations received their guidance, formed their strategies, ran their governments or directed their armies. He said, "We operate on one principle alone." The only way for us to be guided or governed, to make war and survive in this wasteland, is to have the presence of God with us!

Many Christians are completely ignorant of the presence of God. Many ministers and pastors know nothing about the power that lies in the presence of God. Anyone who has not experienced the power of God in his presence has no right to stand and talk about Him because such people do not know him. We all need an encounter, only when we have seen him and touch his glory that our destiny and course can be altered through the hand of the spirit.

> *True believers need to stand with the power and the Anointing in their lives and demonstrate that Jesus Is not some dead, cold, figure hanging on the Cross.*

Having the presence of God with us is worth more than riches or fame or power. We can go anywhere when the presence of God is with us. I can go to many places because His presence is with me even if it dangerous and life threatening. I don't care what direction it is, if the presence of God is there, leading me, that's all I need. If you had no encounter with Him, and all that should die are still alive in you, you have not started in this journey.

In my early days, I used to ask many pastors and ministers that come by about the supernatural, why the nine gifts are not operating in our days, why there is difference during the time of the apostles and our time today. I'm not talking about going after the signs and the miracles, I believe that if we profess to be who we are and what the bible says about us 'These signs shall follow them that believe' Mark 16:17 it is natural that the signs should follow us because this is our spiritual birthright.

These men of God always brush me aside and always tell him that these things are not important and later I realized it is to avoid those questions I asked them because they were ignorant of the working of the supernatural and knew nothing about the anointing. We used to have someone healed of a headache or a pain once in a while but that's all, it will not move into something greater as it is in the book of Acts.

As I seek Him more and more, God was wooing me into the 'secret place' with him. I had to make a choice to separate and sacrifice, separation from all those elements that filled me every day and made my schedule busy and I had to sacrifice and let go many things and choose to be in his presence more than anything.

At one time He told me to get alone with him for three full days, there were no day or night, it's just being with Jesus for 72 hours without food, water and sleep. It was a place I felt as if I had entered into His glory and into that 'secret place' He began to show me many things and teach me the deep things of the Spirit. From then onward I enrolled in the school of the Spirit for 1 year. For the next 360 days, the Spirit of God was my teacher and my secret place was my classroom. Every night when everyone is fast asleep I would attend this classes alone till the crack of the dawn, it was just me and the Lord and it was the sweetest time I had in all my life. At the feet of Jesus, just listening to him, being overshadowed by the spirit, overtaken and fully possessed by Him and diving deeper into the river flowing from the heart of God.

Eze 47:3-4 *And when the man that had the line in his hand went forth eastward, he measured a thousand cubits, and he brought me through the waters; the waters were to the ankles. Again he measured a thousand, and brought me through the waters; the waters were to the knees. Again he measured a thousand, and brought me through; the waters were to the loins.* God took me beyond all words and all my understanding into the deep where I could not walk any more, lose control and surrendered totally to the Spirit.

SWIMMING IN DEEP WATERS

God was telling Ezekiel about wading out into the deep spiritual waters of the Spirit-filled life. What has happened in the modern church is that we have become too afraid to give our all to Jesus Christ. We are afraid because we think that God may require more of us than we are willing to give. We reason within ourselves that, if I don't commit to the work fully then I won't be found guilty of failing in my commitment to Christ. We are just afraid of getting in over our head.

> *The filament in a bulb glows white hot, radiantly. It gives light to all that are in the house but it is the power that flows into it that makes the difference.*

The Prophet Ezekiel was given a vision of a river that springs forth from God's Throne. This river of living water, coming from the Throne of God, is representative of the working of the Holy Spirit in your life. Ezekiel had gone so far from the shore that he could no longer feel his feet touching the ground and could not walk back. He had lost control of everything and when he learn to let go in the deep water, he was swimming in the current of the water. Wherever the river flowed, that was where Ezekiel was going. The current was so strong and the volume of water was so great that Ezekiel was in over his head. Still God was carrying him and there was no danger of the Prophet drowning. God was still in control of the water and of the life of the prophet. Most Christians will never experience the joy, fulfillment, trust and love of God that comes with this kind of commitment because they love the safety of the shore too much.

At one time an apostolic presbyter held a special meeting and invited us to come and be part with that meeting. When we were there during the worship four men carried a paralyzed medium man on a bed and brought him to the service and laid him there at the altar. They told me that this is a witch doctor from the indigenous village that has opposed many people from that village from coming to know the lord. It happened that one day he became very ill and was paralyzed from waist below. The villagers approached him and told him if he will come for the meeting, Jesus will heal him. As he agreed they carried and took him to that meeting hall and as the people worshipped there was a cloud of glory that came upon the congregation. This man began to slowly raise his hands to heaven, the moment he did that the power of God went through his body and he screamed saying 'I feel like fire all over my body' Within minutes, he took off running around the hall praising and magnifying the Lord.

God has no water meter in heaven and Pentecost experience is not a trickle touch of blessing for you to feel good or an anointing to feel the goosebumps. It has a purpose and will continue until the Great Commission has been completed and Jesus returns for His church until we no longer need to evangelize—a continuing and explosive demonstration of God's Spirit till the end of the age. Joel declared that God would pour out His Spirit upon all flesh, this was just the beginning of the work of heaven. The word "pour" does not mean a sprinkling here and there, occasional spills, but revival times. Nobody need chase the Holy Ghost or get him into a corner to persuade him to help. He is chasing us, persuading us, wanting us by His side to make the end times what he means for them to be full of power and revelation of who He is and the work of the cross.

John the Baptist said concerning Jesus, "He shall baptize you with the Holy Ghost, and with fire." God's ministers are to be a flame of fire - a perpetual flame, a constant fire, a continual burning, burning and shining lights. God has nothing less for us than to be flames. We must have a living faith in God, a faith that God's great might and power may flame through us until our whole life is energized by the power of God and the fire of God.

The anointing of the Holy Spirit is given through people to demonstrate God's love and power. Christ means the "Anointed One". Because Christ is in us the same anointing that He had on earth we also have.

(Luke 4:18-19 NKJV) "The Spirit of the LORD is upon me, because He has anointed me to preach the Gospel to the poor; He has sent me to heal the brokenhearted, to proclaim liberty to the captives and recovery of sight to the blind, To set at liberty those who are oppressed; {19} To proclaim the acceptable year of the LORD."

> *God has no water meter in heaven and Pentecost experience is not a touch of blessing for you to feel good or an anointing to feel the goosebumps.*

The 5 results of the Anointing

1. The anointing is given to preach the Gospel to the poor.
2. The anointing is given to heal and restore people.
3. The anointing is given to proclaim freedom to the captives from every bondage.
4. The anointing is given to open blind eyes.
5. The anointing is given to set people free.

The anointing is given to preach the Gospel to the poor, to bring the revelation of God's love, His deity and salvation to those who are seeking.

God's anointing flows to those who are hungry for a touch from His Spirit. The anointing has less to do with the person that it flows through than it does with the person who receives it, and the One who sent it, God Almighty.

When the Holy Ghost comes, He comes to enable us to show forth the revelation of who Jesus Christ is in all His glory, to make Him known as the One who saves, redeems and heals today as in the days of the apostles. The Baptism of the Spirit is to enable us preach good news to the poor, to proclaim deliverance to the captives and recovery of sight to the blind, to release the oppressed, as they did at the beginning, through the power of the Holy Ghost sent down from heaven and with the manifestation of the gifts of the Spirit. Oh, if we would only let the Lord work in us, melting us until a new person in the spirit arises, moved with His compassion and love for the lost!

THE OIL WILL NOT RUN DRY IF YOU'RE OPEN TO RECEIVE A NEW ANOINTING. ASK GOD FOR IT, THEN ASK HIM FOR JARS INTO WHICH THE OIL CAN BE POURED INTO.

If I had to choose one distinctive element of our ministry, it would be that we have been channels of restoration and spiritual renewal for both individuals and ministries. Hundreds and thousands of people who have attended our meetings around the world have testified to a fresh anointing that broke the yokes of the enemy and brought lasting transformations to their lives, their communion with God and their Christian walk especially to the unbelievers. To Him be all the glory!

Elijah has something to teach us about keeping the anointing flowing. Consider his encounter with the widow of Zarephath. He came upon her as she prepares a fire for the last meal she and her son expect to have. When Elijah asks for bread and water, she told him they had ran out of food; all they have left is a handful of flour and a little oil. When that is gone, she and her son will die. This situation illustrates the condition of many believers.

FROM THE DRY LAND

They are God's children, and the oil of the Holy Spirit is in their lives. But their spiritual lives are as good as dead--they barely have any oil in their jugs. They have a devotional life, but it is carried out with great effort, almost as a burden. It is a struggle to pray, to fast and to dwell on his word.

They serve the Lord, but without any joy and fruit of the spirit. Many Christians, are aware

> *It all boils down to one thing, just One thing - How much we want of Jesus and how much we are willing to Sacrifice.*

that their situation is like that of the widow of Zarephath, preparing themselves for their spiritual death. They resign themselves from living Christian lives without joy, power or sparkle. They live their faith without expectation, just waiting to die.

When God anointed you with His Holy Spirit, He didn't give you a spirit of timidity or fear. The oil that descended upon you is the spirit of love, power and sound mind (see 2 Tim. 1:7).

When I was in Bangladesh some years ago, the church had organized a three days revival crusade. For many years they have not experienced any move of God in their local assembly, everything was cold and dead. People had lost the zeal for the lord and passion for the ministry, many were leaving and they had invited us to come. On the first night of the meeting, there were two Muslim women who came in (burqa) *an enveloping outer garment worn by* **women** *in some* **Islamic** *traditions to* **cover their bodies** *when in public.*

One was blind in one eye and the other was partially deaf. At the closing of the meeting, both women came to the front and needed prayer, as they lifted their hands both were struck down by the power of God and the people surrounded them to see what had happened. When they got up, one lady started to jump with great joy because her blind eye was opened and the other lady fell on her knees worshipping Jesus because her ear had opened up.

The next morning we had 32 Muslims that had turned up at the church asking to be prayed for their needs. At the end of the third night, we had a full house of Muslims who came to the meeting with many being blind, paralyzed, deaf, those stricken with cancer and Jesus was there to heal every one of them that came including two Imams (High priest) that were paralyzed due to stroke. We had to collect all those crutches and walking aid at the end of the service because they have no need of them anymore. It was a glorious revival meeting, the church caught the vision and was filled with passion from that meeting and went on to be a thriving group for the Kingdom.

Jesus drew himself to the heart of the people when the multitudes come to him with brokenness he sets them free and healed them all. Luke 6:19 *And the whole multitude sought to touch him: for there went virtue out of him, and healed them all.* The bible says that even before he starts to teach the multitude in Luke 6 He heal them all and then he began to teach the beatitudes -The crowd that was with Jesus on the mountain that day was a healed crowd. None was left behind, none was sidelined and none was denied of their desires to be healed. It is the perfect will that all should be healed and all should be saved and none should perish. When we are delivered we become the vessels for deliverance, when we are healed we become the vessels for healing and when we are saved, we reach others and lead them to the well of salvation. When Jesus met their need physically now they were ready for the meat from Heaven.

FRESH OIL OF ANOINTING

The thing that intrigues me is the word *virtue*. It is an archaic word, used in the times of the King James translators as a synonym for anointing, but today the word *virtue* has to do with things ethical and moral.

In another occasion, the Bible says that when the woman with the issue of blood came to Jesus in Mark 5 and said *"If I am touched by His clothes, I shall be whole." And straight away her blood was dried up, and she felt in her body that she was healed of that plague, and Jesus immediately knowing within Himself that virtue had gone out of Him, turned about and said, "Who touched My clothes?" And His disciples said unto Him, "Thou seest the multitude thronging to Thee and sayest Thou, 'Who touched Me?' " And He looked round about to see who had done this thing, but the woman, fearing in trembling, knowing what was done in her, came and fell down before Him and told Him all the truth. And He said unto her, "Daughter, thy faith hath made thee whole. Go in peace and be whole at thy place."*

> *One man filled with the Spirit and walks in the overflowing is better than a hundred formed committees, which 'keep minutes but lose hours.'*

In this translation, the word is a virtue, but power is relative to virtue, because Jesus felt something tangible *going out* of Him. This implies that it is not a fixed, static amount that He bears at all times, being God manifested in the flesh, but it is relative.

The New Testament Greek words for "anoint" is *chrio*, which means "to smear or rub with oil" and, by implication, "to consecrate for office or religious service"; and *aleipho*, which means "to anoint." A person was anointed for a special purpose—to be a king, to be a prophet, in the new testament beginning the birth of the church this anointing began to flow from the hand of Jesus to the lives of the followers. It is an overflowing tangible glorious presence of the spirit.

The anointing of the Spirit is given through people to demonstrate God's love and power. It is given for the work of the ministry. If you desire to receive this anointing, a fresh anointing of the Spirit upon your life, you must come before the Great Anointer! Remaining in his presence continually and fellowshipping with the Holy Spirit will open the floodgate of the anointing. He alone can give you what you need for the ministry.

And Jesus, immediately knowing in Himself that power had gone out of Him, turned around in the crowd and said, "Who touched My clothes?"

Many times I have been in a meeting when I have sensed the anointing of God falling like a rain. As the warmth of the Spirit has fallen around me I have realized that somebody has reached out to God with their faith and that His healing power is touching their body. I remember one occasion when I was preaching at the end of the service in the United States of America and a woman who was paralyzed from waist below suffering from stroke was instantly healed. As she believed the words

> *A copper pipe cannot boost the water that flows to the tap in our homes if it is clogged. We are to let the living waters flow—just stay unblocked.*

of the Scripture and the teaching on the anointing, the Holy Spirit was able to touch her. I felt the surge of the anointing falling and as I looked I saw her face and her body straightening as God's healing power manifested throughout her body. She stood up completely healed from her stroke and walked to the pulpit all the way from the back and the crowd joined her in worshipping the Lord.

There is no experience like in the second chapter of Acts. It was a mighty visitation of God fulfilling the prophecy of prophet Joel when he spoke about the outpouring of the Holy Spirit that is going to take place at the upper room in Jerusalem thousands of years before it happened. This was the beginning of a mighty move of God that will take over the world through the Holy Spirit, it will spread from Jerusalem to every coast, continents and to the utmost part of this world. Through the outpouring of the Holy Spirit, the anointing will be birth and the church will experience a new baptism of fire that the Spirit of God will carry into the lives of men and women. When the Holy Spirit fell on the 120 of them it exploded from the upper room to the streets of Jerusalem and into every home in that city till the men of the city cry out saying *'what shall we do men and brethren to be saved?'*

As those believers tarried and prayed one more time because they were threatened not to preach in the name of Jesus in Acts 4:31 *And when they had prayed, the place was shaken where they were assembled together; and they were all filled with the Holy Ghost, and they spake the word of God with boldness.* It was a second encounter with the Holy spirit and the breaking of the anointing into their lives. The scripture says they spoke the word with much boldness.

> *The anointing is the invisible finger pointing to the living Jesus, who is the same yesterday, today and forever.*

When there is an overflow of God's spirit you'll be filled with a holy boldness and power to preach the word. The refilling was not only an encounter with the Holy Spirit but of power through the anointing. This encounter released them into the supernatural realm of the Holy Ghost power and boldness.

We all need a second encounter with the spirit of God if we desire to be effective in the kingdom of God. When believers dwell constantly in a life of the overflow it will open up the doors to the nine gifts of the spirit. Every born again believer has an anointing on their lives, however, each of us is responsible for keeping and increasing the level of anointing that is given to us. The presence of God is ever abiding but the anointing is like a current that increases in a river. The scriptures says that we ought to be filled constantly with God's spirit to ensure a fresh flow of the anointing Eph 5:18 *'And be not drunk with wine, wherein is excess; but be filled with the Spirit, Speaking to yourselves in psalms and hymns and spiritual songs, singing and making melody in your heart to the Lord'.*

From Acts 2 the disciples went forward into Acts 4 for a refilling and I believe they didn't stop there as Paul wrote *I thank God, that I speak in tongues more than ye all.*

If they needed it how much more we need them today!

No Stopping

There was a man that came to our revival meeting in Nepal around the mountain area several years ago and he desired to be filled with the infilling of the Holy Spirit for as much he had heard of the spirit but did not have an experience of receiving it. When he came on the first day he was filled mightily and he was trembling and shaking under the power of God for a long time. After the meeting, many church members went to him and congratulated him of receiving this new experience but he told them he didn't receive the spirit yet.

After the meeting, we left that village and travelled to another village that is two hours by car to hold another meeting, he followed us for many miles walking and at the end of service he came to the front and prayed again to receive the Spirit. Again God filled him so gloriously and he was on the floor and speaking in the heavenly language. We left that village and travelled to another place much further than the last place and he followed us by foot and came again to the meeting we were having service and again God filled him mightily, he was overshadowed with God's glory for more than two hours. From there he went on to be a mighty warrior for the kingdom of God winning many to the Lord.

God used him in a special way because he tarried in the presence of God to be filled, refilled, and refilled again and again. A nation in need of the apostolic revival needs someone that is drenched with the Holy Ghost Fire! Just one man or one woman can make the difference.

Luke 3:16 "John answered them all, saying, 'I baptize you with water, but he who is mightier than I is coming, the strap of whose sandals I am not worthy to untie. He will baptize you with the Holy Spirit and fire.'"

5 SECRET PLACE OF THE MOST HIGH

The glorious working manifestation of the Spirit of God in preparing the church for the latter days outpouring with the demonstration of his resurrection power as never experienced before is going to take place before Jesus returns for his people. Our greatest desire of the hour should be seeking his wonderful face, his sweet presence, and his tender loving arms.

Once you have a foretaste the sweetness of his presence and the fellowship in the glory, you will long forever to be in that place. There is no other better place than to be in his holy presence beholding his face.

(Rom 8:35,37-390) *Who shall separate us from the love of Christ? shall tribulation, or distress, or persecution, or famine, or nakedness, or peril, or sword?, Nay, in all these things we are more than conquerors through him that loved us. For I am persuaded, that neither death, nor life, nor angels, nor principalities, nor powers, nor things present, nor things to come, Nor height, nor depth, nor any other creation, shall be able to separate us from the love of God, which is in Christ Jesus our Lord.*

The main important aspect of our walk with God in deep closeness is to desire to continually be in his presence as David said in Psalms 27 *One thing have I desired of the LORD, that will I seek after; that I may dwell in the house of the LORD all the days of my life, to behold the beauty of the LORD, and to inquire in his temple.* The one thing becomes his main thing that is to seek after the presence and face of God continually because his presence brings Joy, strength, comfort, love and I'm transformed every time I enter his presence.

Moses was convinced that without the presence of God in his life, it was pointless for him to do anything. When he spoke face to face with the Lord, he said, *"...If thy presence go not with me, carry us up not hence"* (Exodus 33:15). He was saying, *"Lord, if your presence is not with me, then I'm not going from this place. I won't take a single step unless I'm given the assurance that you're with me!"*

Refreshing in God's Presence

In our modern days if the church has the manifested presence of God in their midst, there won't be any hustle or bustle, sweating or striving, working things out with our efforts. The worship meetings won't be hurried along, with three or four songs, an offering and a short sermon because everybody has to rush back home or to a mall or food store to get their meal. Instead, there will be a calming peace, a quiet rest, a place of reaching into the depth of God and allowing the spirit of God to lead and control the moment and everyone who walks through the doors will feel the difference that heaven have touched us! This doesn't mean a church service can't experience loud praises or exuberant worship. On the contrary, I believe those things are often the result of a people who are in the glory. There will be a manifest explosion of worship and praise because God has stepped in with his angels in that place. When God began to move and step in the whole environment and atmosphere will change, once the glorious presence is in the midst of the church it will be alive.

> *The fire that fell on Mount Carmel is the same fire that fell in Acts 2. But it has a different effect. The fire of God tests each one, what they are. It fills believers with dancing joy but scorches the godless.*

The same is true for every individual believer. If you have the presence of Jesus in your life continually experiencing him in your walk, you will enter into God's divine order. You'll have a peace that passes every understanding and a calm in the midst of every storm, with no fretting or anxiety, no running to and fro seeking counselling and advice, no sense that the bottom is falling out. You'll live at peace, knowing God has everything under control.

When the children of Israel were in the wilderness, God showed his presence to them when he visited them through a cloud. This cloud was a physical manifestation of God's agreement that he will go before his people. It came down and covered the tabernacle at day and at night there will appear fire on the tabernacle to signify that he is with them. It was their assurance that God is with them and before them and acted as their guide for every undertaking. When the cloud moved, they moved, and when it stayed, they stayed. The people didn't have to hold committee meetings or to try to figure out which direction they have to go. Their confidence and guide was in that visible cloud of God's presence.

SMUGGLERS OF THE WORD

Today, that same cloud of his presence hovers over us in the secret closet of prayer. It waits every day to envelope us with its joy and peace. It will lead you, empower you and give you peace.

When I was travelling to Thailand by train God spoke to me and said 'I want you to go to Nepal', there are people everywhere in that train but because we have accustomed to tune into the voice of God in the secret place, you recognize his voice even in the nosiest and bustling places, he speaks without any geographical barriers. I said 'Lord I cannot go because this nation is undergoing civil riots and it is very dangerous'.

He not only ask me to go but also instructed me to carry bibles into this nation. Later we found ourselves travelling inside Nepal with my wife together with hundreds of bible piled up in the back of our vehicle. There were many soldiers of both from the government group and the moist (communist) group who flooded the city and the streets but his presence covered us as we took each step from the airport right through the country churches. As we started our 16 hours journey into the mountain by a four wheel drive with another companion, we were warned by the local not to open our mouth and speak or answer to anyone along the way. We were carrying the bibles and if we were find to be with these bibles, we will be taken away by the Maoist regime and probably ending up losing our lives.

It was a long journey from the capital city Kathmandu and there were so many checkpoints by both of these groups. In every checkpoint, our Nepali companion would speak to them in their own dialect and they will let us go but as we came almost to the end of our journey toward the evening, we were stopped at one of the checkpoints and the officer in charge demanded to know why we were there. Even after a long explanation from our guide the officer was not satisfied and demanded to know what we are carrying and ordered us to open the trunk of the car, hundreds of the bibles are in the trunk. As the driver flunk open the trunk, the soldier turned everything upside down in the trunk and after looking for so long he said on top of his voice "You may go now" As we started back the journey our hands were up in the air praising the lord for sending his angels to blind the eyes of these soldier at the checkpoint as that they could not find a single bible in that trunk even though we had them piled up in the trunk of the car.

> *Prayer and Worship is the prerequisite to the miraculous realm.*
> *A man can alter his destiny in the secret place*

Your secret closet can be anywhere Daniel found the secret place three times a day. Dan 6:10 *Now when Daniel knew that the writing was signed, he went into his house; and his windows being open in his chamber toward Jerusalem, he kneeled upon his knees three times a day, and prayed, and gave thanks before his God, as he did aforetime.*

The secret closet of pray is a designated time and place to be alone with God. It is in this environment believers develop intimacy with

God. This is where we are revived and molded to be a people after his own heart.

It's a wonderful thing to be shut in with God in this secret place, developing a consistent prayer life. God promises that as you become a seeking, praying servant, his presence will break forth in your life as a fountain - closing and opening doors and working his divine order all around us. Something even greater than this will take place: God's presence will lead you into a revelation of his glory.

There is a difference between God's presence and his Glory. Most Christians know his presence - his great works in their lives - but few knew and had experienced his glory. In Exodus, we're given a glimpse of this difference between this two: *"Then a cloud covered the tent of the congregation, and the glory of the Lord filled the tabernacle"* (Exodus 40:34).

The apostle Paul writes that all believers' bodies are the tabernacle of God: *"Know ye not that ye are the temple of God, and that the Spirit of God dwelleth in you?"* (1 Corinthians 3:16). Like the children of the Israelites who lived under the cloud of God's presence, we need constantly to be covered under the covering of God's presence.

Moses began to seek after for a continual dwelling in his presence: *"...that I may know thee..."* (Exodus 33:13-14). And God answered him, *"...My presence shall go with thee, and I will give thee rest"* (verse 14).

> *Believers are not ordinary people with religion as a hobby. The world has its absorbing enthusiasms, and its "fans", But Christians are not raised but born in the spirit and water.*

Just as Moses' requested, it would be quite enough for most believers today. We all want the presence of God - leading us, guiding us, blessing us. Yet there is something else that was missing, just having the assurance of

God's presence wasn't enough for Moses. He knew there was more. And he cried out, *"...I beseech thee, shew me thy glory"* (verse 18).

Even though God said that *'Thou canst not see my face: for there shall no man see me, and live'.*

But this prayer of Moses stands entirely alone. It is a category unto itself. No other request can be compared to it. God's glory is the sum total of who he is. It is God's power, his wisdom, his justice, his mercy, his holiness, his love, every other attribute of his character. God's glory is the shining forth of who God is in his essence.

God showed Moses his glory. But it didn't appear as probably some of us has hoped for. No, God expressed his glory in a simple revelation of his nature: *"The Lord passed before him, and proclaimed, The Lord, the Lord God, merciful and gracious, longsuffering, and abundant in goodness and truth, keeping mercy for thousands, forgiving iniquity and transgression and sin..."* (34:6-7). God's glory was a revelation of his goodness, mercy, love and compassion!

The anointing that comes from the overflow of the presence of the Holy Spirit is tangible, the ability of God given to an individual personally to fulfill God's purpose, mission, ministry to manifest his love and mighty deeds, whereas the presence of God is sovereign manifestation of God in a person which manifests in the infilling of this baptism of the spirit and continues after that. However, you can't have the anointing without the presence of the Holy Spirit. Jesus spoke about this tangible anointing in Luke 8:46 *'And Jesus said, somebody hath touched me: for I perceive that virtue is gone out of me'.* He felt something tangible leaving his body when that woman with the issue of blood for twelve years touched him. We read of this woman in the Gospel of Luke who was sick and defiled with her illness - a chronic hemorrhage of blood (Mark 5:26-34). She was so defiled she would render anybody unclean she fingered. But she was desperate for help and came for the Master's touch-- behind Jesus to touch Him, feeling she had no right to get help. It was by stealth. If Jesus was like any Pharisees, she could expect an explosion of protest - "How dare you touch me?" She touched Jesus. Instantly the fountain of her blood was stopped.

Then it came - Jesus knew! "Who touched me?" He demanded BECAUSE HE KNEW THAT THE ANOINTING WAS ZAPPED OUT OF HIM. She sneaked away, her little statue hidden by the big men. She was frightened. Everybody wondered if He was pretending to know, and what He would say. He had been in the Temple and been furious with anger. This little lady knew that He knew, and feared that awful rage. Eventually, she had to own up. She came trembling and dare hardly look up at Him. She clutched her dress at her chest and in a guilty whisper admitted, "It was me. I'm sorry -. Forgive me. I know I should not have done it." Jesus looked down at her weak little shoulders and her terrified eyes. Then she saw His gaze, full of unspeakable compassion and grace. He said, "Don't be frightened! Go in peace. Your faith has made you whole." She took that anointing that was on him and made him say *"somebody hath touched me."*

THE POWER OF THE WORD OF GOD

In our early mission trip days to Nepal, we would bring in many bibles without the communist Maoist group finding out as it was illegal for someone to own a bible during the moist regime in Nepal. Somehow some of these bibles had reached to the most interior and to the churches in the mountain areas and after three years later when I went back to Nepal, we met an Old Nepali women of God, one of the recipients of the bibles. She was illiterate but she was full of God and full of his presence. You can feel the love and compassion through her sweet aged eyes, they were as bright as a shining star that is radiant with God's love. Many years ago she was diagnosed with Leukaemia, all her family forsook her due to the burden of looking after her. She was given only a few months to live and in her struggle with this sickness

> *David said he did not have a sword or a shield and yet declared he would cut Goliath's head off. True faith attempts what unbelief would never dare to tackle.*

someone from the church had given her a bible and told her about Jesus and read the passage where it reads *He sent his word, and healed them, and delivered them from their destructions. Psalms 107:20.* She would place the bible to her heart and claim the word as God sending the word to heal her.

After a couple of weeks, she was completely healed of this Leukaemia and many Hindus began to come to the Lord. She was attending the mountain church and as usual during their weekend service that church was raided by the moist insurgents and they demanded cash ransom. When the pastor mentioned that they have no money because they are poor, the militant group began to beat up everyone and on the way out the head of the militant noticed this old woman was embracing her bible to her bosom and was sitting on the floor at the exit of the church.

That man began to grab hold of that bible believing that it must be something that is very valuable. She began to cry out loud and said Sir please don't take the bible from me, this is the only possession I have, I don't have a house, I don't have a family and children, the only thing I own is this bible. Please don't take it away from me, this is my life" That man did not bothered of the cry of that old woman and kicked her with his boots and took the bible away from her. She began to weep and weep and no one could console her broken heart, everyone left back home that day but that woman stayed back at the altar and began to pour her heart to the Lord.

After three days she being at the altar, suddenly she felt someone touching her from the back and as she turned back to look, it was the same militant leader that took her bible away. This time he came to her side knelt beside her and said "mother I could not do anything for three days, I've lost my peace and my sleep." Please tell me about this God your serve that is in this bible" She began to testify about Jesus and that was the day the angels in heaven rejoiced over that one soul that has persecuted the church like Saul in the book of Acts and saw the light of Salvation and was redeemed by the hands of grace.

Behind His salvation is all of the fullness of God, His wisdom, omniscience, infinite love and justice. When He saved us it was the eternal burning of His loving heart. All that we see of His power in creation is the power that shook Pharaoh on his high throne but when we see him manifested in the flesh he shook the Roman Empire from center to circumference. This power of Him manifested to destroy the works of the enemy from whom creeping demons fled in terror at the mention of his name; it all lies behind our salvation. To save us took the flame of His love, His passion in the garden of Gethsemane so intense that brought the sweat of blood to His brow. We are saved by a so great love manifested through his salvation.

The main important thing in my walk with Jesus, I strive to continually dwell in his sweet presence because His presence brings, joy, peace, strength, direction, courage, love and I'm transformed every time I enter into his presence. There's no place better to be than in the presence of the Almighty under the shadow of his wings *Psalms 91:4*

He shall cover thee with his feathers, and under his wings shalt thou trust: his truth shall be thy shield and buckler.

THREE DIMENSIONS OF DEEP PLACES WITH GOD.

First Dimension

When we are born again in him through the water and through his spirit as it is written in John chapter 3. *There was a man of the Pharisees, named Nicodemus, a ruler of the Jews:*

The same came to Jesus by night, and said unto him, Rabbi, we know that thou art a teacher come from God: for no man can do these miracles that thou doest, except God be with him. Jesus answered and said unto him, Verily, verily, I say unto thee, Except a man be born again, he cannot see the kingdom

> *Christianity has a lot of meaning to many people—just a part-time interest, a Sunday club, or psychological comfort for old age. But that is not it. Christianity is to know and have Jesus in you, its revelation and relationship with the one that rose from the dead.*

of God. *Nicodemus saith unto him, How can a man be born when he is old? can he enter the second time into his mother's womb, and be born? Jesus answered, Verily, verily, I say unto thee, Except a man be born of water and of the Spirit, he cannot enter into the kingdom of God. That which is born of the flesh is flesh, and that which is born of the Spirit is spirit.* This is just the beginning of the new birth experience. This is a place of adoption by the spirit of God whereby we cry 'Abba Father' *For ye have not received the spirit of bondage again to fear; but ye have received the Spirit of adoption, whereby we cry, Abba, Father (Rom 8;15)* In this first encounter we are filled with his first love that trust us into a deep relationship with Jesus as never been experienced before.

Second Dimension

We enter into the second dimension when we are touched by his resurrection power and quickened in the spirit. *Rom 8:11 But if the Spirit of him that raised up Jesus from the dead dwell in you, he that raised up Christ from the dead shall also quicken your mortal bodies by his Spirit that dwelleth in you.* In this place, we are drawn deep into an intimate relationship and walk with him. Nothing is more important than pleasing the master and establishing a close fellowship with him. We enter in this place seeking his face rather than his hands, we feel what he feels for the lost and carry the burden for those that are in the darkness.

> *A deep place with God is where there is perfect communion, perfect fellowship, and pure intimacy between our spirit and every dimension of God's spirit.*

We are brought into a deeper dimension of God's presence, our soul hunger and thirst for God in the same way a deer pants for the sustenance of water. "Intimacy with God is found only in the realm of the spirit." A deeper dimension of God's presence involves waiting, longing, thirsting, seeking and knocking. *David wrote, "O God, thou art my God; early will I seek thee: my soul thirsteth for thee, my flesh longeth for thee in a dry and thirsty land, where no water is; To see thy power and thy glory, so as I have seen thee in the sanctuary" (Psalm 63:1-2).*

Intimacy with God is found only in the realm of the spirit. There is a place of deep anointing, deep presence, and deep intimacy with God where "deep calleth unto deep" or the spirit of man calls unto the spirit of God.

It is a place that is so precious and pure that every part of our being is consumed by the presence of God; a deep place where there is perfect communion, fellowship, intimacy between our spirit and every dimension of God's spirit.

Deep calleth unto deep at the noise of thy waterspouts: all thy waves and thy billows are gone over me (Psalm 42:7).

Third Dimension

This is where the river of God flows into us and to others. *Those who live according to the flesh have their minds set on what the flesh desires, but those who live in accordance with the Spirit have their minds set on what the Spirit desires. ⁶ The mind governed by the flesh is death, but the mind governed by the Spirit is life and peace. Rom 8:5-6.*

The moment our passion and desire takes a shift from the carnal nature and transform into the passion of the spirit and the mind of God, He will open up the wells of the living water to flow freely into our lives. We will be filled completely with the divine nature of God for the task of the kingdom. The burden and love for souls and the kingdom will be more than fulfilling our own desires. We live, move and have our being in him. Nothing satisfies us than doing his will and being filled with his presence continuously. There is perfect harmony, perfect oneness. As we bask in the glory of His wonderful presence, our own spirit begins to fellowship with Jesus and crying out, *"That I may know him, and the power of his resurrection, and the fellowship of his sufferings, being made conformable unto his death"*

Jesus Christ is same yesterday, today and forever, the anointing is just the same, the Pentecost experience is just the same and we are to look, desire touch and explode in the same experience of the early church. A heart that is aflame for God cannot be quenched by the cries of the dead formalism from the spiritual content, it cannot be blown away by the winds of spiritual apathy nor can it be choked out, smothered out or stomped out by the lure of the worldliness and materialism. The scriptures says that *'I count all things bot loss for the excellency of the knowledge of Christ Jesus (Phil 3:8).*

Jer 20:9 Then I said, *"I will not make mention of Him, Nor speak anymore in His name."But His word was in my heart like a burning fire Shut up in my bones;I was weary of holding it back, And I could not"*. How Jeremiah was torn with this inner tension -- of fear and a dislike of proclaiming the truth, because it only subjects him to ridicule and scorn; and yet when he resolved to quit he found he could not, because the fire of God was burning in his bones and he had to say-"But *His word* was in my heart like a burning fire Shut up in my bones. Can we afford to hold back when the world around is marching straight into hell? There are wars and rumors of wars, immorality in high places and reaching the altitude as never before Rom 1:16- *'For I am not ashamed of the gospel of Christ: for it is the power of God unto salvation to every one that believeth'*

> *Without the Truth (Acts2:38) and the Spirit(Acts 2:2-4), Christianity is reduced to 'religion', which is no more effective than the Old Testament system and the priesthood before the age of Pentecost.*

When we see people are bombarded with sin and surrounded with the influence of hell everyday; pulling them away from the knowledge of Jesus, we need to pray for a burning burden for the lost, oppressed, those that are inflicted with sickness and diseases.

We need to step out in the anointing of the Holy Spirit and the authority that has been invested in us as believers and allow the overflow of the of the living waters from the wells of salvation to reach the lost and only through the anointing we can break every chain of bondage that bounds the people.

Isaiah 10:27 And it shall come to pass in that day, that his burden shall be taken away from off thy shoulder, and his yoke from off thy neck, and the yoke shall be destroyed because of the anointing. There is a yoke-breaking anointing. God tells us in the bible that "*I will make a way where there is no way*". There is a facility of escape. Man's word is not final because man is mortal. A yoke is something that places the destiny of a man in the hands of the enemy. A prisoner cannot eat what he pleases or go anywhere he wants to. In Acts 12:6 we are told that Peter was in prison between two soldiers bound with TWO chains and there were keepers who kept the prison door!!! The only thing that could free the destiny of Peter was a divine intervention.

Jesus broke the yoke of infirmity that bound him up for 38 years in the life of the man at the pool called Bethesda (John 5:8). This man had diverse, multi-dimensional yokes but one glorious day Jesus walked to that pool just for him and said to him "*rise, take up thy bed, and walk!*" The problem of 38 years got solved in 38 seconds when the hands of immortal God reached and touched this mortal crippled by the pool.

Jesus stood in all five offices. He was an apostle (Hebrews 3:1). He was a prophet (Mark 6:4; Acts 3: 22-26) Peter said that Jesus was a prophet whom Moses spoke about. He was an evangelist as we can see from Mark 1:4 that He went about preaching the kingdom of God. He was a pastor as John 10: 11 says that He is the good Shepherd. He was known as a teacher in John 3: 2 where Nicodemus said that "we know that You are a teacher sent from God." The Lord Jesus Christ was anointed to stand in all the five offices.

As each one of us called into different positions and offices, each office carries different anointing. Sometime a person can carry up to 3 offices but there is a relation between the offices and the anointing that is vested on us.

Some time ago when we were in India some believers took us to a remote village in India to visit and later to hold a revival meeting in that place. However, that village has been under the control of a witch and to enter into that village you have to pass through her house. Many Christians never approached this village due to the threat the witch imposed on them.

On one evening when the meeting was going on this lady tried to cast a spell and put fear on those people that want to attend, preventing them from come for any meeting. As there was no electricity, lighting at the meeting was done with car batteries and without any tents, many came and were touched, healed and set free that evening. There was a man that became lunatic and spent his days at the grave yard with torn clothing, he would sleep at the grave because that witch at the village did something terrible and he lost his mind and spent many months outside, the grave was his home. When someone brought him to the meeting he was set free completely. Later he and his wife gave their lives to Jesus. That witch that was tormenting that village, all of a sudden, fire struck her house and she took off running and left that village and never came back. There is a church constructed at the place and many that do not know the Lord gave themselves to Jesus because the believers began to exercise what Jesus had given to them.

When you close the door of your personal prayer room behind you, the door of heaven opens up. When the 120 disciples locked themselves in the upper room of prayer for about ten days, the windows of glory were unlocked and the Holy Spirit rained upon them with fire. (Acts 2)

All around the world, there are prayer rooms, upper rooms, in churches, colleges, even in administrative offices everywhere. A prayer room is a powerhouse of God!

Exodus 40:9 - And thou shalt take the anointing oil, and anoint the tabernacle, and all that [is] therein, and shalt hallow it, and all the vessels thereof: and it shall be holy.

6 TOUCH OF HEAVEN

There is power in the written and spoken word of God, I believe every word that is written and spoken will ignite and propel faith to release the miracle we are longing for. This faith will manifest itself through its fruit and demonstration of the supernatural. The scripture says without faith it is impossible to please him and all things are possible to him that believeth.

An electric lamp is the most transparent object. It's just a mere ornament. In itself, it is useless for anything. Unless and until someone turn on the switch we could not see the effect of a light bulb. There could be a thousand volts of electricity power supply sitting idle and seemingly connected to that bulb but until it's allowed to flow into the light bulb it's useless. As the small object called the switch controls the power supply so does our faith that connects to the supernatural power of God. Until and unless we turn on the switch called 'faith' and faith ignites the miracles, the supernatural will not be evident. It gives light to all that are in the house.

Heb 11;6 But without faith it is impossible to please him: for he that cometh to God must believe that he is, and that he is a rewarder of them that diligently seek him. Mark 9:23 Jesus said unto him, If thou canst believe, all things are possible to him that believeth.

We read in the scriptures what took place in the gospel of Mark, there was a man who brought his son to Jesus because his son was demon possessed. Since Jesus was on the mountain the man talked with the disciples instead. The son had a spirit that made him mute and whenever the spirit would seize (attack) the boy it would throw him down and the boy would foam at the mouth, grind his teeth, and become rigid.

The man asked his disciples to heal the boy, but they could not heal him. Jesus came down from the mountain after being transfigured with Peter, John, and James with him. When he came down from the mountain and came to his disciples he saw that there was a crowd around them and that the Scribes were disputing with them. The boy had definite manifestations of a spirit that caused him to be thrown down to the ground, foam at the mouth, grind his teeth, and become rigid.

As soon the master walked into their midst, there was commotion and the crowd ran toward him while the scribes were questioning the disciples of the act they were involved with that boy and Jesus asked them what was going on. One of them replied saying the disciples could not deliver the child from his condition and Jesus said in disappointment "You unbelieving generation," Jesus replied, "how long shall I stay with you? How long shall I put up with you? Bring the boy to me."

Apparently, Jesus was not pleased with what he saw. The passage says that he replied to them. Who is "them?" I would have to say that his remarks were directed at his disciples since they were the ones who were expected to heal the boy. The man exercised

> *There could be a thousand volts of electricity sitting idle and could not produce the light from the bulb because its switch was not turned on, we could be sitting and waiting for a miracle but it will not walk into our life without switching on the element of 'Faith'*

some faith by bringing the boy to the disciples so it is doubtful that Jesus' remarks were addressed to him.

Notice the emotion suggested by Jesus' statements. He stated that the disciples were unbelieving (faithless). Without faith, it is simply impossible.

In many instances, there are two different type of faith that is involved in producing healing and deliverance. Firstly it is the faith of the person that is seeking for a miracle and secondly the faith of a believer that is ministering to that person for a supernatural touch. Either of the two could open up the wells of miracle and in the absence of the both, we will be as the disciple with that young lad. Later when they came to the master and enquired privately why they were unable to have the authority over the demonic spirit, the Lord said firstly because they doubted and secondly to possess the measure of faith to speak to the mountain it must be birthed out of prayer and fasting. I've heard of an old Pentecost preacher that was used by God so mightily during his time, thousands of miracles were wrought through this man even to the raising of many dead persons. When at one time it was asked of him how he could be able to perform all these miracles, he simply said "I cloth myself with prayer and the word from morning till late noon and then when it's time for me to step out of my house to find someone to pray for the element of faith is at work."

A DOCTOR IN NEED

At one time in our home fellowship in Malaysia, people was gathered for the evening meeting and many people were in that small house with the majority being from the Chinese background. A couple wheeled in a lady in a wheelchair to that meeting, she was paralyzed from waist below and could not walk. She is a doctor from Calcutta India and was married to a Malaysian many years ago and due to a car accident, she was paralyzed. She came into that place with her face twisted with many doubts. This looks like an impossible situation on the outside but the Lord was ready for her.

As we lifted our voice in prayer I was led to read Is 53:1-3 *Who hath believed our report? and to whom is the arm of the LORD revealed? For he shall grow up before him as a tender plant, and as a root out of a dry ground: he hath no form nor comeliness; and when we shall see him, there is no beauty that we should desire him. He is despised and rejected of men; a man of sorrows, and acquainted with grief: and we hid as it were our faces from him; he was despised, and we esteemed him not*

When I got to the fifth *verse "But he was wounded for our transgressions, he was bruised for our iniquities: the chastisement of our peace was upon him; and with his stripes, we are healed"* she began to shout I'm healed, I'm healed, I feel heat passing through my legs. As people lifted her from the wheelchair she began to take few steps and walk and slowly she was walking for the first time after many years on her own.

The word of God took hold of her and lifted her faith from where she had been. It was a place of no hope and despair but when faith gripped her heart she was ready for her miracle. God touched her limbs and she walked around the place clapping her hands. All the pain around her neck and the countenance of her face changed from gloom to radiant with God's glory. The crowd burst into Joy and the atmosphere was charged with faith and exuberant worship and praise of the people.

> *The only chance faith will ever get is now, It can't operate in heaven where there is nothing at risk. Faith is our auto-pilot for the flight, not for when we landed and walk the crystal floor of glory.*

Faith cometh by hearing and hearing the word and God's word releases faith in our hearts not to only believe but to act upon what we believed.

In order for us to be saved, we need to first hear the word and take the word in obedience through the baptism of water and the spirit. If we keep on hearing and hearing and not committing to the obedience of that wor, we will not be partakers of salvation, there will be no fruits that will be manifested. It goes same with healing and miracles, when we hear the word, we need to act upon the word in faith without wavering.

Once in a prayer, God revealed to me in a vision that every time a prayer ascend to the gate of Heaven for a particular need of healing or miracle touch of God, He appoints his angels to carry the miracles to earth in a golden platter. As the angel approach the believer to hand over the miracle healing in a meeting congregated, all of a sudden the environment changes when the believer says "Now is not the time for me to receive this miracle," and there was another believer that proclaimed saying "It's God's will for me to carry this infirmity and I accept it." The angel that brought those answered prayers for these saints could not deliver them as it was blocked out from them through their unbelief and their words that stopped the miracle from taking place and the angel return back with much sadness to the throne room unable to conclude the assignment he was given because these saints failed to receive what was brought to them. And then I heard the voice of the Lord saying, look at these saints that have lost their miracles because of their unbelief, in order for them to receive, it only takes a leap of faith. They were so close yet so far.

> *A pair of frail hand grabbed Peter's, pulled him back on his feet again, onto the surface of the sea. That was Jesus. "Why did you doubt?" He asked (Matthew 14:31). He still asks us the same question. "Why do you doubt?"*

The angel came and spoke to Mary of this miracle. The miracle happened when Mary answered (in verse 38), *"Behold the handmaid of the Lord; be it unto me according to thy word."* Mary simply believed and accept the miracle when it was spoken even though it was against all the law of nature. When God creates, He speaks it into existence by His Word, the Rhema word.

God did all His miracles by the spoken Word. In Genesis, He created the world by the spoken Word. Hebrews 11 tells us, *"Through faith we understand that the worlds were framed by the word of God, so that things which are seen were not made of things which do appear."* The important point is that your miracle is involved in your word.

Many Christians put prayer above all and believe that if you pray, it will happen. Prayer is like water and fertilizer that you put on the seed. But, without planting a seed, watering is useless.

And then the Lord said the keys to receive any miracle that has been transported from heaven is firstly, to believe that it is for them and it is their season for a miracle and secondly to proclaim with their heart and words that they are ready to receive it now.

God is sovereign and orderly. He doesn't do one thing this time and another thing another time. God created this world and everything physical around us, and the physical world is orderly created through his word.

FAITH THAT MOVES MOUNTAIN

We were invited to the capital city of India sometimes ago to hold a revival service in that area for it was a new work. The church went out and displayed banners and posters of this special meeting and sent invitations to those who need healing and deliverance. We were having service for three nights and in all those nights many first time visitors came from Hindu backgrounds from the villages. We had to hold the meeting in a bible school venue to accommodate all those that would come. Every night many were receiving physical healings and deliverance from demonic possession.

On the third night we had an overwhelming crowd that came from the villages on trucks and buses to this meeting and by the time the meeting ended it was almost midnight, there were few people remaining at that place with the believers including a 19 year old Hindu girl name Rupa. She was dumb and deaf from birth, her brother had accompanied her to this meeting and remained very skeptical about the whole thing. We asked her what was wrong with her, her brother said that she is dumb and deaf and wanted to be prayed for.

As she came forward, we prayed and she collapsed to the floor, when she stood up the brother was very angry and said "Look what I told you these Christian people nor their Jesus can help you" and started to walk out from that place. This girl suddenly began to scream "Jesus, I can hear I can hear" and she could speak few words that were not very clear. Her brother stood in total amazement and later both of them came to the altar and surrendered their lives to Jesus. Rupa came to the meeting with an unwavering faith in Jesus and holding to the word spoke to her, she began to hold on to it in her very desperate situation. Even though her brother could not believe for a miracle, Rupa had fully pledged her faith on the master hand as the only healer and deliverer. Whenever you have burn your bridges of doubt and begin to walk in the path of faith, no need saying what this Jesus will do, for He is moved every time when he sees someone reaching out to him in total complete faith.

THE FRAGRANCE OF HIS PRESENCE

We are promised that where two or three are gathered together in the name of Jesus, He is in the midst of them:

"For where two or three are gathered together in My name, I'm there in the midst of them." (Matthew 18:20)

I believe from experience and from Scripture that Jesus loves to manifest Himself in our midst and one of the ways in which He does so is through the fragrant aroma upon His garments. I recall one meeting in the Philippines Island where an unsaved person came forward for salvation and for the baptism

> *Compared to the resources open to us through the spirit of God. Our natural abilities are a drop in the ocean. When we sing "Fill my cup Lord". A cup full? But God promises us rivers, waters to swim in!*

of the Holy Spirit. After which he was been filled with the baptism of the spirit and he said he had never been in such a meeting. He thought that the singing was wonderful, people healed and delivered and the prayers were good, but he told us that he just loved the perfume with which they sprayed at the altar!

I have received testimonies and known people to go from meetings smelling this fragrance around them for several days before they realized it was the fragrance of the presence of the Lord.

It is a powerful witness of God's presence upon us. Some people question the Scriptures in this regard. However, I accept these Scriptures without question. Those of us involved in the deliverance ministry know too well. The horrible stench that accompanies demons on many occasions. As demons are being cast out of people the stench often surrounds us. Thus we rejoice to know the beautiful fragrance of the one who walked on this earth and said 'I'm the truth and life' which comes upon us as we gather together in the name of Jesus Christ.

The fragrance that surrounds the believer is a witness of His presence with the believer. This is how we are separated from the world. I believe also that the same fragrance from the Spirit of God can be among the believers when they gather in the name of Jesus and that this is a further expression of the meaning of the Scripture:

Now thanks be to God who always leads us in triumph in Christ, and through us diffuses the fragrance of His knowledge in every place. For we are to God the fragrance of Christ among those who are being saved and among those who are perishing. (2 Corinthians 2:14-15).

In Songs of Solomon, the Shulamite woman declares that God's love is better than wine*: "Because of the fragrance of your good ointments, Your name is ointment poured forth"* (Songs of Solomon 1:3-4). *Where the name of Jesus is exalted in adoration, the stage is set for you to enter into a secret place in which you smell that anointed ointment that's poured forth in our midst.*

Looking at the passages about the **anointing** oil, which was fragrant—and unique. Exodus 30:23-25 instructs, "Also take for yourself quality spices—five hundred shekels of liquid myrrh, half as much sweet-smelling cinnamon (two hundred and fifty shekels), two hundred and fifty shekels of sweet-smelling cane, five hundred shekels of cassia, according to the shekel of the sanctuary, and a hin of olive oil. And you shall make from these a holy anointing oil, an ointment compounded according to the art of the perfumer. It shall be a holy **anointing** oil."

The blend of herbs was used for the **anointing** oil and *only* the anointing oil. This was a type of the anointing of the Holy Spirit. A.W. Tozer, a 20th-century, preacher, put it this way:

"The fragrance of the **anointing** oil was unique. If someone went near an Old Testament priest, he could say immediately, 'I smell an anointed man. I smell the holy oil' the aroma, the pungency, the fragrance were there. Such an **anointing** could not be kept a secret. It exposes to everyone that come in contact with."

When we are born again, the **anointing** abides: *"But the anointing which you have received from Him abides in you, and you do not need that anyone teach you; but as the same anointing teaches you concerning all things, and is true, and is not a lie, and just as it has taught you, you will abide in Him"* (1 John 2:27).

This is true, and yet there is another experience of the **anointing**—that fragrance of God, the sweet-smelling aroma of His presence. One way to get to that place is through deep **worship**, opening your heart up completely to Him, asking for nothing and ready to receive anything He might offer, and pursuing His heart with all of your heart.

> *Pentecost is not a token of death but a trophy of resurrected life and victory. The true sign of a living Lord is living fire from heaven. We need the scholars and the elites but how much better it is when it comes to the people filled with the Holy Spirit.*

When we walk in love and constantly overflowing in his presence, we give off His scent. Moved by the **Holy Spirit**, Paul wrote, *"Therefore be imitators of God as dear children. And walk in love, as Christ also has loved us and given Himself for us, an offering and a sacrifice to God for a sweet-smelling aroma"* (Eph. 5:1-2).

Faith is an inward operation of that divine power of the spirit that lives in us and can lay hold of the things that are not seen in the substance of a human eye. Faith is a divine act through the spirit of God. The scripture says he that come to God first and foremost must believe (*But without faith it is impossible to please him: for he that cometh to God must believe that he is, and that he is a rewarder of them that diligently seek him.* (Heb 11:6) faith is active and not dormant, faith is the unseen hand of God in an adverse situation, faith never fears, faith lives in the midst of greatest conflict. When everything fails faith will stand strong. God operates through his spirit that dwells in us and transforms the natural to supernatural. We are His life and the members of his body. When we are filled to the brim with his spirit and his word dwells in us so richly there is no place for the carnal but only the mighty things in the spirit of God. As one man of God said 'The word of God is the anvil that has worn-out many hammers! Spiritual Patriarchs believed that no sacrifice was too great. They were builders of relationship with God and they were sold out!

James 1:6 But when you ask, you must believe and not doubt, because the one who doubts is like a wave of the sea, blown and tossed by the wind.

7 OVER FLOWING RIVER

As we look into the life of David, he didn't just want to be a man of obedience and having an intimacy with God alone but he pursued after him to see the power of God released to his nation through his life. *"O God, thou art my God; early will I seek thee: my soul thirsteth for thee, my flesh longeth for thee in a dry and thirsty land, where no water is; To see thy power and thy glory, so as I have seen thee in the sanctuary. Psalm "63;1-2.*

Here we are looking at a man that God calls 'A man after my heart' There is a place where he will bring you into the deep places with him to show his glory and power and the moment we are exposed to his attributes and majesty, God will cloth us with his glory for his purpose. Every gifting and empowering begin with a deep intimate fellowship with the king.

To be a person after God's heart, we must follow what David did and pursue God until the master begins to empower us with his glory and be established on this earth as it is in heaven. David was the only one in the written scriptures that had a double fold office as king and a priest. David also believed in the priesthood of the king. He and his sons were priests "forever" after the order of Melchizedek (Ps. 110:4). In the tabernacle, David saw the manifestation of God through the thunder and lightning, later in the fire. He wanted this manifestation to continue to all the congregation of Israel when he said *"To see thy power and thy glory, so as I have seen thee in the sanctuary."* A dwelling place of God speaks of a place where God's power is openly manifested to his people. David was not satisfied just to seek him privately and to experience God's glory, he wanted a demonstration of God's power in all Israel that the nation around them would fear the Lord.

When the Lord first called us to go into Bhutan many years ago, he gave us dream and burden of this Buddhist nation that rejects every element of Christianity and the truth from reaching them. The Lord further directed us to bring bibles into this country and reach these wonderful people for the kingdom. We put our lives on the line of danger when we took hundreds of bibles there. We have heard of many Christians that were thrown into the dungeon and were tortured for preaching and reaching the people of Bhutan and here we are, standing outside of the border of this Dragon Kingdom with our bibles, as we were praying God send a Bhutanese young man and his friend around nine o'clock at night and offered to take us on their motorbike inside of this country. Later we found out he was a believer. My wife was on one bike and I was on another bike with all the bibles. We passed through the border security without been asked to stop as though the angels had blindfolded them and these officers could not see us and the bibles we were carrying. Once inside this country, we walk in the park and in their town laying the bibles on every benches and sidewalk and prayed that God will bring the hunger for him to his word. The next day as we went in the daytime a couple approached us and took us by their hands and brought us into a building and we had to climb five floors up to a secret chamber close to the roof and there we met an Indian missionary couple that were living secretly and were praying for two weeks that God would send someone to them and for some bibles. When we met them they were on their knees weeping because they were cut off from the outside world and were hiding in that place for months, fearing for their lives because they reached out to some of the teachers at the local Bhutanese school. We all lifted our hands and worshipped Jesus quietly and the sweet presence of the Lord came into that small room and filled us all with his glory. We were all taken into the cloud of glory as we tarry in the presence of Jesus. Later they took us to the small village school and introduced us to these teachers that were so hungry for the Lord. We prayed for them and return with joy because God has founded his people in this nation where the gospel could not be preached openly.

When God sees an available vessel that is ready for the master's use He will move heaven and earth just for that one person to be filled, anointed and equipped through his spirit so that His Kingdom may be established on the earth.

The Christian circle may seem to have many competitors if we classified it lower than what is it, just a part-time interest, a good cause, a Sunday gathering, or psychological comfort for old and the lonely - all merely incidental. But that is not what it is all about than identifying with Christ. Christianity is Christ in me the hope of Glory, the comprehensive purpose and power of life and resurrection of Jesus.

> *God opens up the wells of salvation to all those that are hungry, He promises us rivers. When you or I step out beyond where we are, we will stand at the threshold of great usefulness. A door of service fit for a King stands open before every believer.*

No religion big or small, has anything like that to offer, even if you search this whole globe. When the master came arrayed in the flesh and blood he did not come to form another religion but to call out those that are lost and to empower those that are ready for his purpose. Jesus said "I have come that they may have life and have it more abundantly. "As we found this fullness of life in Him we want to impart this wonderful journey to others.

When we look at the beginning of David's passion, it is engrafted from his heart to the scriptures. In Psalms 40:8 he said *"I delight to do your will my God and your law is within my heart"* As we look in the third expression what it means to be a man after God's heart; it's a heartfelt pursuit for the fullness of God's power and his purpose for this generation.

BEING THE PERSON ON ONE THING.

When Mary was expecting Jesus to visit her at her place she had made up her mind on one thing, to sit at the feet of the master and to be engulfed with his love and heartbeat. She didn't worry much the place he need to be comfortable or she needs to prepare him a meal. This was the only opportunity she is going to have with the messiah and she didn't want other things to take her place. When Martha eyes met with his, Jesus said one thing, just one thing is needful and Mary has chosen the good part.

As one preacher said "The world is waiting for someone to walk through her streets, her hamlets, her villages, her countryside to demonstrate the passion and true dedication of the love, passion and power of this resurrected One--Jesus Christ.

When we were invited to hold a revival meeting for the Apostolic Circle in Nagaland, we had to drive almost 16 hours from its capital city to the other side of the border connecting to Burma. We were exhausted when we arrived at almost 2am in the morning, my back and all my joints were aching as we hit the cold temperature climate of 5°C and I told myself that I will not be able to do this again and I'm not coming back to this place. The next morning before the gathering, the leaders introduce me to a man that had come from Burma. He walked three nights and three days through the jungle alone to reach this place taking the risk of being moulded by wild animals. He came because he was hungry for something deep just as Mary longed from the Lord and he did not return disappointed. He was filled with the baptism of the Holy Spirit in all three days and the last day he got drunk in the Holy Ghost and he went back with a new zeal to build and plant a new church in Burma. After meeting him, I repented, terrible conviction gripped my heart and I told the Lord even if you want me to come back a thousand times I'm willing Lord.

The world has so many unworthy passions. The question of eternity is "Do you love me more than these?" (John 21:15). The love of Jesus is backed by a million reasons. It ought to infuse all we do, where we go and what we say and what we think. It need not be an unruly shout in the marketplace and in a monumental cathedral, but it can be a subtle perfume that everybody can smell.

DEEPER INTO THE DEEP

Deep calleth unto deep at the noise of thy waterspouts: all thy waves and thy billows are gone over me

Psalms 42:7.

In essence, this is the Spirit of God reaching deep into the spirit of His people, bypassing all that which would attempt to impede that sweet communion and fellowship God so passionately desires to have with us.

It is in part, living out the words of Jesus when He said; "God is Spirit, and those who worship Him must worship in spirit and truth" (John 4:24). The word deep in Psalm 42:7 includes in its meaning; great. All of God; The Great I Am, lives in all of those who have received and filled with His spirit and He has great things in store for us as we respond to the deeper things of His Heart and the Kingdom.

When we receive the Barnabas call to go into Nagaland back in 2011 through a vision, I began to read as much as possible about this land and to my surprise there was hardly any missionary that went into Nagaland because its borders were closed to foreigners to protect the local tribals. Nagaland is a mountainous state in northeast India, bordering Myanmar. It's home to diverse indigenous tribes especially those that have migrated from Mongolia. The Naga tribes were often engaged in internecine warfare, and the practice

> *The question of eternity is "Do you love me more than these?" (John 21:15). The love of Jesus is backed by a million reasons. It ought to infuse all we do, where we go and what we say and what we think. It need not be an unruly shout in the market place and in monumental cathedral, but it can be a subtle perfume that everybody can smell.*

of head-hunting - decapitating captives and civilians for religious ceremonies. There is no proper road connecting to those districts in this land and moreover, the toilets and sanitation were very bad. When I read about all that I went to the Lord and said 'No Lord I'm not going to Nagaland, I've been to many difficult places but to Nagaland, it's a no for me'. I was afraid of even coming back alive from this place and that's when the presence of the Lord withdrew from me for 3 weeks completely. I was in a dry and dead place with God, everything was still and dark and there was no life in me. I can live without food, water and many other things but not without the presence of God.

Then one evening when I went to the master and repented of my stubbornness and said 'I will go, Lord, even if it will cause my life' then all of a sudden as the psalmist said 'all thy waves and thy billows are gone over me' God just opened up the lit poured out his presence. It was like I was standing under the mighty currents 100,000 cubits per second of water falling from the Niagara Falls. It went on for hours as I got drunk in that presence.

In my disobedient and fear, I have shut down the pipeline of God's mighty presence and glory that was avail to me all the time. "Deep calls unto deep." Only a call from the depths can provoke a response from the depths.

Nothing shallow can ever touch the depths, nor can anything superficial touch the inward parts. Only the deep will respond to the deep. Anything that does not issue from the depths cannot touch the depths. If nothing comes from the depths, the walk we have is just superficial. When we take a glance of Peter and John being present at the empty tomb examining the grave-clothes of the risen Christ. It was not a question anymore when Jesus said if you destroy this temple I will rise it again in three days. The words of Jesus began to ring again in that cold and dark tomb as a reminder but it never ever crossed in their minds that they are the ones to display the blood-marked wrappings as evidence of his resurrection to other disciples, like holy relics to be kissed and touched.

They had better things to do and obligations to fulfill but they choose their time waiting in the upper room until the promise of the prophet of old is fulfilled and the fire to fell.

Pentecost is not a token of death and shame but a trophy of life and victory. The true sign of a living God is living fire from heaven came down from heaven, unlike the fire that fell at Mt Carmel to display God's glory. As Peter and John looked at the disciples, even enemies could tell that they had been with Jesus. We need scholars, the elite and the nobles how much better glorious it is when it comes from those that are filled with the Holy Spirit; inspired and ignited with the fire of the anointing.

When we step out in the fullness of His anointing and authority, God is going to bring us into the deep waters allowing the rivers of life to flow into the lives we are reaching.

Wells, waters, streams, cisterns in the bible and river refer to our walk and exposure to the Spirit of God and his working power.When Jesus was at the feast In the last day, that great *day* of the feast, Jesus stood and cried, saying, *"If any man thirst, let him come unto me, and drink* and he further said *He that believeth in me, as the scripture hath said, out of his belly shall flow rivers of living water,* He was not only referring to the initial experience and infilling of the Holy Spirit but he was revealing the overflowing presence of this spirit in a believer's life, it can be as rivers, mighty rivers that flow out and touch every kindred tongue and nations of the world.

> *We do not defend the Gospel and the preaching of the truth with high profile security system and fences. The truth is best defended when it is preached to those that are in darkness. Only then its true light is displayed, the captives are freed and chains are broken.*

The five levels of Ezekiel's vision (Eze 47:1-10) and prophecy give believers an understanding how the presence and the power of God can be increased through many levels

¹Afterward he brought me again unto the door of the house; and", behold, waters issued out from under the threshold of the house eastward: for the forefront of the house stood toward the east, and the waters came down from under from the right side of the house, at the south side of the altar.

² Then brought he me out of the way of the gate northward, and led me about the way without unto the utter gate by the way that looketh eastward; and, behold, there ran out waters on the right side.

³ And when the man that had the line in his hand went forth eastward, he measured a thousand cubits, and he brought me through the waters; the waters were to the ankles.

⁴ Again he measured a thousand, and brought me through the waters; the waters were to the knees. Again he measured a thousand, and brought me through; the waters were to the loins.

⁵ Afterward he measured a thousand; and it was a river that I could not pass over: for the waters were risen, waters to swim in, a river that could not be passed over.

⁶ And he said unto me, Son of man, hast thou seen this? Then he brought me, and caused me to return to the brink of the river.

⁷ Now when I had returned, behold, at the bank of the river were very many trees on the one side and on the other.

⁸ Then said he unto me, These waters issue out toward the east country, and go down into the desert, and go into the sea: which being brought forth into the sea, the waters shall be healed.

> *Jesus said I'll send the promise of the father, referring to the Holy Spirit. He promised the abiding presence of His Spirit. His power is the secret of the believers walk. It enables the weak to be strong, the feeble to be mighty and the faint to be victorious. Without the Holy Spirit Christianity is just another religion*

⁹ And it shall come to pass, that every thing that liveth, which moveth, whithersoever the rivers shall come, shall live: and there shall be a very great multitude of fish, because these waters shall come thither: for they shall be healed; and every thing shall live whither the river cometh.

¹⁰ And it shall come to pass, that the fishers shall stand upon it from Engedi even unto Eneglaim; they shall be a place to spread forth nets; their fish shall be according to their kinds, as the fish of the great sea, exceeding many.

Level 1 – To Behold

Ezekiel being the prophet of God facing the temple and beholding the waters that flows from the temple. When Ezekiel saw the vision (573 BC), there was no temple standing in Jerusalem. Solomon's temple, which had previously stood there, had been destroyed thirteen years earlier by Nebuchadnezzar, when he conquered Jerusalem and deported the citizens to Babylon. This means that Ezekiel was not seeing Solomon's temple. He was looking at the church of the New testament that were being filled with the baptism of the spirit. As he stood there he was amazed gazing at the waters that were flowing out of the temple knowing this was something that was not normal to take place. He just stood there watching the flow of this water. In this level believers become spectators of the move of God. The believers don't have the understanding nor the revelation that they possess within them when they received the infilling of the spirit. They are just spiritual babies contented with what they have and promised to them. They fail to activate and release the power of the spirit of God through prayer, fasting and the word. They are moved to see how this flow of the spirit operates through others. Instead of being involved in the move of God and the work of the spirit, they wait on others and just watch what God is doing through other vessels.

We were invited to visit the nation in south Tibet some years ago, as we arrived at that place I did not go with any warm clothing as I was not informed about the climate of that place that is freezing cold at 3°C but reaching to this place I was shaking and shivering as the cold drill itself to my bones. It was about 6pm and some of the leaders took me to a wooden hut at the foot of a hill. I was wearing 3 shirts and two pants to withstand the cold but I could not help but shake all over while we walked to that place.

Arriving at the place we found about 30 believers gathered together for a time of worship and to hear the word from a stranger that has come from thousands of miles. I had an interpreter with me to translate to their local dialect. I came to understand that none of them had the infilling of the Holy Spirit and never heard of the Holy Spirit. While we were seated at the place I was offered a hot cup of tea to warm me up but within a minute the tea became cold due to the weather. In that wooden hut, there were gaps between the wooden planks and the cold wind from the mountain was blowing into that room as it frozen the place further. We just lifted our hands to the Lord and worshipped as the service began with one young teenager playing the guitar. As we started to worship we began to move into something that is so glorious and everyone was so intense into the presence of God. The glory of God just flooded that place with an intensity. All of a sudden I felt something warm around me as a heat and I was feeling as I was walking waist deep in a hot water tub. I looked at the interpreter and asked "Do you feel what I'm feeling" He said yes. I asked him further is anyone burning firewood outside to keep the place warm, they told me there is no fire outside and then I knew the Fire of God fell in that place and it was simply glorious. The young teenage boy was filled mightily with the Holy Spirit and he flung the guitar to the ceiling and began to dance. People getting the Holy Spirit without me laying hands on them and I've not delivered the word yet and this was happening.

> *What Jesus paid on the Cross is translated into our lives by the Holy Spirit. What He paid so dearly for, the Spirit of God confers on us. We can't be a Christian without the work of the Spirit nor without His indwelling presence. It is a pure river of His presence that flows from His throne because of Calvary!*

The young musician began to touch the people and God was filling everyone, at the end of four hours in the presence of God all thirty believers were on the floor worshipping the Lord. The crippled walked, the blind received sight and all sort of sicknesses were healed under the power of God. Nobody want to go home, no one wants to say anything, it was deep waters from the throne of God that has flowed in and filled this place. It was heaven's glory touching earth moment.

Level 2 – Ankle Deep

Going on eastward with a measuring line in his hand, the man measured a thousand cubits, and then led me through the water, and it was ankle-deep at this place prophet Ezekiel experienced that the water that is flowing out from the temple began to increase and it was up to his ankle. He was standing in the midst of the water feeling the little current passing him but he was still in control of his position. In this place, believers have a desire to be used by God but are consumed by their own desires and worldly ambitions. Even if they are filled with the spirit of God there is no depth they can go due to lack of consecration and dedication of a fully surrendered life.

They have little experience with God and satisfied with their position with God having their own abilities and the spirit of God being suppressed in their lives because of carnality and worldliness. Their self-dependency robbed them of their potential in the Lord and their anointing to be victorious.

Level 3 – Knee Deep

In this place prophet Elijah was brought where he experienced the water has increased much and the water rose from his ankle to his knees. He realized that certain times he loss control of his standing position but regains his position because he is still able to. At this place, believers become complacent of their position with God. They will experience the move of God in their walk with him but they hold back their commitments and try to have a balance of both the world and their walk with God. Even though there might be evident of the power of God once a while but it is not constantly flowing from them to others.

When we were having revival services in Indonesia, God was moving very deeply in all the nights in their bible college graduation service. There was a young man that has travelled all the way from Sumatra to attend this bible college and at the end of the graduation, the lord was calling him into a deep walk with him and also into the ministry. He had his own plans made out to carry his father's business when he returned but God was restructuring his future. He would lay on the floor night after night groaning in the spirit as God overshadowed him. All the three nights the spirit of God would fell on him in such a powerful way but he would resist the hand of God knowing where he is calling him to. On the final night I told that young man that if he would surrender God would elevate him to a place where thousands would be won to the Kingdom but if he would reject what God is doing, the enemy is waiting to deceive and to destroy him. That young man stayed all night at the altar in prayer and surrendered himself and went out to be one of the finest and God anointed minister for the kingdom.

> *The ways of Jesus is too great for our small minds. His way is not our way neither are His thought to ours. He has never fitted anybody's pattern book, leaving the scholars of His day dithering and lost. We don't call Jesus the Son of God because He measures up to what we think He should be.*

The world has always had things so enticing to offer to divert our focus from the master's call but nothing in this present world can compare to the glorious things he has in stored for his people.

But as it is written, Eye hath not seen, nor ear heard, neither have entered into the heart of man, the things which God hath prepared for them that love him (1Cor 2:9)

Level 4 – Waist Deep

The waist deep experience that the prophet had was so remarkable that he could feel the current that is flowing all around him but he still could feel the ground with his feet. At times he was pushed out of the way and almost fell to the flowing water but he was able to stand with both feet. At this point the believer could be active with his involvement at his local assembly and even having a ministry at the church, but they are unwilling to surrender all and still dependent on their ability and talent. The measure is half of the body length indicating a halfhearted believer. They come to a place where it is hard to surrender everything to the Lord, their family, career, finance while they are in the same kind of ministry. The duty of serving God becomes more than a vocation day in day out without a deep relationship with Jesus.

Level 5 – Overwhelming Deep.

Finally the prophet was given the opportunity to experience an overwhelming flow of the water that flooded him from the tip of his head to the soul of his feet. He has been to the ankle deep, knee deep, waist deep but to be exposed to this kind of flow is extraordinary. He could not crawl, walk and run in the water anymore but he had to swim or he would have been drown and his feet was not touching the ground. There is no other options but to let go and surrender to the overflowing current of the water. He had to make a choice either to swim or drown.

This is the place where every believer will be surrounded and submerge in the power of God. They will lose all sustainability of the flesh and completely live in the overflowing life of the spirit of God. Is a place where they will experience the supernatural and the manifestation of the nine gifts of the spirit without measure. They will not only demonstrate the gifts of the spirit but the fruit of the spirit will follow them. It will be so evident and continually manifesting in their walk with Jesus

Is 11:2 And the spirit of the LORD shall rest upon him, the spirit of wisdom and understanding, the spirit of counsel and might, the spirit of knowledge and of the fear of the LORD;

8 THE 7 FACETS OF GOD'S SPIRIT

Eph 3:19
And to Know the Love of Christ, which passeth knowledge, that ye might be filled with all the fullness of God.

Paul prayed for the saints in Ephesus that they might be "filled to the measure of all the fullness of God." The believers in Ephesus were saved, as we use the term, and had received God's Spirit but they were lacking something.

God is always searching for a person whom he could illuminate and enlarge himself through that individual until there is nothing that hinders His presence and power from flowing out to the world through him or her. You will have the anointing of God flowing through you when God's heart touches another person's heart through you. The anointing of God comes from the Holy Spirit and He flows as a river of love, from the throne of grace, through the lives of believers, bringing life to all that receive His touch.

God anoints people that love Him more than they love their own lives, and that love others as themselves. As we open our hearts to love others God's anointing flows through us. When we close our hearts to others especially souls and grieve the Holy Spirit the flow stops.

The anointing of the Holy Spirit is given through people to demonstrate God's love and power. Christ means the "Anointed One". Because Christ is in us the same anointing that He had on earth we also have.

(Luke 6:19-20) *And the whole multitude sought to touch Him, for power went out from Him and healed them all.* Then He lifted up His eyes toward His disciples, and said: *"Blessed are you poor, For yours is the kingdom of God".*

(Matthew 5:3) *"Blessed are the poor in spirit, For theirs is the kingdom of heaven". The term poor here is the Greek word, ptochos which carries the implication of being a beggar, in this case, a spiritual beggar longing for the Spirit of God.*

The anointing can be stifled if the people refuse to receive it from the one that God is sending it through.

Things such as pride, envy, bitterness, and unforgiveness against an anointed person can prevent the receiver from accepting it. The anointed person must go to people that are hungry, open and ready to receive it.

> *A cross consists of two beams—one horizontal and one vertical. Horizontal is our relationship with the Master and Vertical is our relationship with others. Without the both we will not have the Seal of Love- true love for the Lord and burden for souls.*

(Matthew 13:57-58) So they were offended at Him. But Jesus said to them, *"A prophet is not without honor except in his own country and in his own house."* Now He did not do many mighty works there because of their unbelief.

The anointing is sacred, the anointing is the overflowing presence of the Holy Spirit, and all believers in Christ have the anointing of the Holy Spirit as long they are filled with the baptism of the spirit and constantly refilled and flowing in

the spirit of God. We must be careful what we say about our brothers and sisters in Christ. Our tongues can the greatest weapon of the enemy to destroy the anointing that God put in us.

We can quench the spirit of God when we speak evil of our brothers and sister and carry gossip and talk evil of those that are of the household of faith especially pastors and ministers. And the greatest tool the enemy will use to stop and make you sin against the Holy Spirit is when you blasphemy against him, when you deny your experience with him.

(Matthew 12:31) *"Therefore I say to you, every sin and blasphemy will be forgiven men, but the blasphemy against the Spirit will not be forgiven men"*.

I know a young man that was from a Hindu background, the Lord found him at the point when he was at his crossroad. One day we received a phone call from his family that their son is dying because he has cut both wrists and was bleeding to death. He was at the point of taking his own life because of involvement in drugs. They rushed him to the hospital and was given intensive care and the doctors lost all hope. As we prayed the Master walked into that cold and dark room with his warm loving hands at the hospital room and restored that young man back to life. Later he was baptized in Jesus mighty name and God miraculously filled him with his spirit. He went to the bible school and pledge to serve the Lord but some years later due to his involvement with an unbelieving partner whom he later married, he left his walk with the Lord.

He became cold as a block of ice to everyone and denied the experience he had with Jesus and he lost his salvation. He was only 31 years old when he had a cardiac arrest and was taken back to the same hospital and he was at the verge of death but this time he lamented saying he can't come back to the Lord as he had profane against the Holy Spirit and spoke evil of his experiences with the Spirit, there is no turning point anymore for him as he could no longer feel God's presence even if he would cry and wail and call on God.

God's presence had left him just like in the life of Saul and another evil spirit had taken over him

Men are constantly on a stretch, if not on a strain, to devise new methods, new plans, new organizations, new ways to advance and progress the Church and secure enlargement and efficiency for the gospel and call it revival. This modern end time trend has a danger attached to it, we have the tendency to lose sight of the real purpose we are called to be the vessels of God and then sink man in the plan of organization and church growth. God's plan is to make much of the man after His own heart and image, His own plan through the working of the spirit, far more of him than of anything else. Men are God's method made before the creation. The Church is looking for better methods; God is looking for better men filled and equipped with His Spirit.

> *A Fuse, tiny as it is, it transmits the awesome power generated in power stations to our homes. Without it, every appliance is useless, unable to draw from that power. And once connected, the fuse itself cannot help but show the effects of the power surging through it. It warms up!*

The glory and efficiency of the gospel are staked on the men who are called to proclaim it. When God declares that "the eyes of the Lord run to and fro throughout the whole earth, to show himself strong on behalf of them whose heart is perfect toward him," he declares the necessity of men and women and their dependence on them as a channel through which to exert God's power upon the world.

What the Church needs today is not more machinery, better plans and methods, not new organizations or more and novel methods, but men who are full of Holy Ghost and anointing—men of prayer, men mighty in prayer that know how to walk and live in the spirit. The Holy Ghost does not flow through methods but through men. He does not come on machinery but on men. He does not anoint plans, but vessels - men and women of anointing.

The believer is the golden pipe through which the divine oil flows and it flows from the source—Jesus the anointed One. The pipe must not only be golden and unclogged, but open and flawless, that the oil may have a full, unhindered, un-wasted flow to whom it is designated.

God created us for a purpose. Each individual was created according to God's plan and purpose. Nature is created by God to declare the glory of God. The Bible says; **"Heaven declares the glory of God. The sky proclaims the work of His hands", if so we have a higher purpose and calling than the nature itself.**

When we were in Nepal on our third trip to this nation, we were holding a three days revival services in a beautiful city call Pohkara. There were many that needed the baptism of the Holy Spirit and we had over one hundred people from that city and the surrounding mountain area that came to seek and to be prayed for the infilling of God's spirit. On the first day some of them were filled when God began to pour out his presence on these hungry souls. But something happened on the second day as we delivered the word, faith began to rise among the people and such a thirst for the presence of God overwhelmed the people and even before we called them to the altar the people rushed to the front to seek and to be filled with the baptism of the Spirit.

As the people were praying, suddenly I noticed something that was happening in the crowd, there were a lot of commotions and the crowd in the middle were moved and as I looked carefully there were about fifteen young children that were pushing the adults around them to get to the front. These young children were from the

> *Jesus spoke about "Rivers of living water" for us. (John 7:37 38, NKJ) Not lake, but rivers fresh, lively, sparkling, abundant, and unending and always flowing and giving life. Some people live for what comes out of a lake. When we shift our focus from the lake to the River mentality we are repositioned for something that is powerful never-ending and that could change the world.*

age of nine to fifteen, something happened and they were very desperate for God to touch them. This event reminded me of the woman with the issue of blood in the bible (Luke 8:43-48).

Everyone that was praying in the front and behind them was suddenly interrupted and could not pray anymore and I thought to myself what is going on with these children, maybe they are trying to hinder the service. But to my amazement, all those fifteen young children were weeping and the moment they got to the altar, they raise their hands and were worshipping the Lord with all their might with deep moving of their hearts. As they were worshipping the power of God fell and hit all the fifteen of them and within few seconds they were all speaking in tongues and some were on the floor overshadowed by the glory of God. It didn't stop the power of God that fell on them then it moved to the crowd and touched the congregation and filled them too with the baptism of the Holy Spirit. We had almost all the church speaking in tongues as they were filled mightily. This was one of the few times that I've witnessed where the whole congregation was filled with the baptism of the spirit of God.

These children because of their hunger for God had opened up the wells of the Living water bringing down the presence and the glory of God into their midst and allowing themselves to be the conduit for God to flow to all those around them. They were instrumental vessels that God could use to bless others. Age doesn't matter for God to use you as long as you have the unquenchable thirst for God, you will be filled. "**Blessed are those who hunger** and thirst for righteousness, for **they** shall be filled" (Matthew 5:6)

Hunger and thirst are natural expressions of the basic human desire and need for food and water. One of the clear indicators that something is wrong physically is when we lose our appetite. It is the same spiritually. To hunger and thirst for God is at the very root of our being. It's the way God made us. When there is no hunger for the presence of God, it is an indicator that something is wrong spiritually.

On another occasion when we were in Pakistan holding a four days revival meeting in a certain town, people were gathered from all the villages to attend this meeting and over hundred people that needed the infilling of the Holy spirit were there. For three nights so many miracles took place, we saw the blind eyes opened, the crippled walked, the deaf hear and many that came with sickness were healed but none received the infilling of the spirit yet. But on the last night when the service began there was a heavy thunderstorm and the rain hit the ground so strongly. All the bamboo poles that were supporting the tent collapsed to the ground and the people were standing in an open air totally drenched in the rain, small children as young as two years old were standing with their parents with hands lifted up to the heavens. We had lost all electricity power, no light, no sound system that was operating and we all just stood in the dark ground totally soaked in the rain but no one moved from that place, no one ran to take cover. I just told the people to lift their hands and praise the King of Kings and the word was preached to the people and within minutes we had the whole crowd in one voice praising Jesus. As we worshipped the Lord something marvelous began to take place, God was sending his heavenly rain and filled all those that need the baptism of the Holy spirit. None was needing anything anymore and lacking anything for everyone was filled for a long period of time on that cold dark night. This was one of the best services around the globe we experienced and the minister was the Holy Spirit.

> *The purpose of God's word is to lead us and inspire our faith in him. The Bible is a manual of faith in God that has been given to us "so that the man of God may be thoroughly equipped for every good work" (2 Tim 3:17). It is God's voice in the burning bush calling out to us—urging us to surrender our doubts, abandon our misgivings and follow him.*

"On the last and greatest day of the Feast, Jesus stood and said in a loud voice, *'If anyone is thirsty, let him come to me and drink. Whoever believes in me, as the Scripture has said, streams of living water will flow from within him"* (John 7:37-38).*"Come, all you who are thirsty, come to the waters; and you who have no money, come, buy and eat! Come, buy wine and milk without money and without cost. Why spend money on what is not bread, and your labor on what does not satisfy?"* (Isaiah 55:1-2).

King David was a man who knew what it meant to live under pressure. As the king of Israel, he knew the pressures of leadership. The higher and more responsible the leadership position, the greater are the pressures. And David knew the pressure of problems. During his reign, his son, Absalom, led a rebellion against him. David and his loyal followers had to flee for their lives.

During that time David spent a short while in the northeastern side of the wilderness of Judah before he crossed over the Jordan River. In that barren land, fleeing for his life from his own son, feeling disgraced and rejected, with an uncertain future, David penned the beautiful Psalm 63.

Psalm 63
O God, thou art my God; early will I seek thee: my soul thirsteth for thee, my flesh longeth for thee in a dry and thirsty land, where no water is;
To see thy power and thy glory, so as I have seen thee in the sanctuary.
Because thy lovingkindness is better than life, my lips shall praise thee.
Thus will I bless thee while I live: I will lift up my hands in thy name.
My soul shall be satisfied as with marrow and fatness; and my mouth shall praise thee with joyful lips:
When I remember thee upon my bed, and meditate on thee in the night watches.
Because thou hast been my help, therefore in the shadow of thy wings will I rejoice.
My soul followeth hard after thee: thy right hand upholdeth me.
But those that seek my soul, to destroy it, shall go into the lower parts of the earth.
They shall fall by the sword: they shall be a portion for foxes.
But the king shall rejoice in God; every one that sweareth by him shall glory: but the mouth of them that speak lies shall be stopped.

In those time of pressure, rejection, loneliness David found his heart attached close to God. When everything was empty and void, he clinged on something that was eternal, something that was solid and assured. It was the presence of God that comforted him and with one hand holding to his harp he wrote down this beautiful Psalms with the other hand, that had passed down to generations.

Psalm 139:7-13;
Whither shall I go from thy spirit? or whither shall I flee from thy presence? If I ascend up into heaven, thou art there: if I make my bed in hell, behold, thou art there. If I take the wings of the morning, and dwell in the uttermost parts of the sea; Even there shall thy hand lead me, and thy right hand shall hold me. If I say, Surely the darkness shall cover me; even the night shall be light about me. Yea, the darkness hideth not from thee; but the night shineth as the day: the darkness and the light are both alike to thee. For thou hast possessed my reins: thou hast covered me in my mother's womb.

Through His indwelling presence, God shapes our character and allow us to bear the fruit of the Spirit (Galatians 5:22). The gifts of the Holy Spirit will operate through us as a result of His indwelling presence. It is the Spirit in the life of a believer that gives and operates these gifts.

God's manifest power is for special events. It does come either heralding the commissioning of a man for a special task, to hand down a special message, or to deliver someone precious to Him. It is often temporal in nature but leaves permanent glorious testimonies to those that receive it.

> *Christianity allows an ancient creed but follows a living God, the Messiah. You can't sign on the dotted line in a church journal book to make you a Christian or enroll in a Christian group to make it to heaven. You can't just utter a formal sentence to make you a believer. It is a matter of the heart. You got to be born again, justified through your faith.*

When it happens, we see an instant change in the life of its recipient. Hardly has anyone experienced God's manifest power and remain the same. It appeared to many who were terminally sick and they received instant healing.

In Acts 9:3-9 we read of Saul's encounter with the manifest presence of the Lord that changed everything about him. When Jesus prayed on the mountain he was transfigured as the manifest presence came down (Luke 9:29).

Presently, we often witness God's power flowing in Christian meetings, touching lives, healing many and delivering others from the yokes of the devil. My sincere desire and prayer are that every believer will develop his and her relationship with God to the point that they will begin to witness the manifest presence of God in his favour that allows the power of God to flow.

These are the seven facets or manifestations of the Spirit of God in the believer's life when we are filled with His spirit and fullness of God:

1. The Spirit of Justification: *"...you were justified in the name of the Lord Jesus and by the Spirit of our God."* We are all justified because of God's grace and by our faith in obedience to his word, and it is the Spirit of God who draws us and empowers us to acknowledge Jesus as our One true living God (John 17:3) This is the first work of the Spirit when one is born again. (1 Corinthians 6:11) And such were some of you. But you were washed, but you were sanctified, but you were justified in the name of the Lord Jesus and by the Spirit of our God.

2. The Spirit of Sanctification:
2 Thessalonians 2:13, "...God from the beginning chose you for salvation through sanctification by the Spirit and belief in the truth." Sanctification is the process of God's grace by which the believer is separated from sin, purified by a life lived in the Spirit. *(2 Thessalonians 2:13)* The fruit of the Spirit will begin to manifest as we yield to the process of sanctification. To

sanctify someone or something is to set that person or thing apart for the use intended by its designer. A pen is "sanctified" when used to write. Eyeglasses are "sanctified" when used to improve sight. In the theological sense, things are sanctified when they are used for the purpose God intends. A human being is sanctified, therefore, when he or she lives according to God's design, will and purpose.

3. The Spirit of Intercession: **Romans 8:26, "Likewise the Spirit also helps in our weaknesses. For we do not know what we should pray for as we ought, but the Spirit Himself makes intercession for us with groanings which cannot be uttered.** The Spirit of God, in the first place, a Spirit of prayer. He was promised as a "Spirit of grace and supplication," He was sent forth into our hearts as "the Spirit of adoption, whereby we cry, Abba Father." He enables us to say in true faith and growing apprehension of its meaning, Our Father which art in heaven. "He maketh intercession for the saints according to God." And as we pray in the spirit, our worship to God seek to be, "in spirit and in truth." Prayer is just the breathing of the Spirit in us; power in prayer comes from the power of the Spirit in us, waited on and trusted in. For praying the effectual, much-availing prayer of the righteous man, everything depends on being full of the Spirit.

> *We cannot simply preach with the anointing unless we preach the Word. He is committed to fulfill the promises of His Word. The Holy Spirit is not just a sweet influence or the gentle ambiance in a church, but He will confirm the spoken word. That is His eternal association. When we preach the Word, the Spirit is in it.*

4. The Spirit of Life: **Romans 8:2, "For the law of the Spirit of life in Christ Jesus has made me free from the law of sin and death."** This is the Spirit of adoption (Romans 8:15) which makes us the sons of God (Romans 8:16-19). We can now live in the

resurrection power of Christ where the operation of the gifts of the Spirit is normal and cause our lives to become supernatural. The Spirit will give life to our mortal bodies as well as those who we come in contact with. Where we go we bring and project life to everyone we come in contact with. Healing and strength will come into our bodies of flesh (Romans 8:11) as the anointing increases, giving us a glorified body in that day of His return.

5. The Spirit of Truth: **John 14:17 *"The Spirit of truth, whom the world cannot receive because it neither sees Him nor knows Him; but you know Him, for He dwells with you and will be in you."*** The truth will set us free. The truth will bring revelation knowledge as we are taught by the Holy Spirit. The Spirit of truth will reveal Jesus as One True God to us (John 15:26). "You have an anointing from the Holy One, and you know the truth" (1 John 2:20). The Holy Spirit is the spirit of truth, and that means we will be kept from error and deceptions from the enemy as long as we are led by the spirit and the truth. The spirit of revelation will be given to lead us into all truth and reveal the kingdom to us. Deception will be removed, and the lies destroyed.

6. The Spirit of Deliverance: **Matthew 12:28 *"But if I cast out demons by the Spirit of God, surely the kingdom of God has come upon you."*** It is by the power of the Holy Spirit that we are delivered from sin and by that same Spirit demons are cast out and the powers of darkness are defeated. The spirit of God will break and loose you and your family from any vows made; from any person or any occult or psychic sources, and any demon coming through the bloodlines in Jesus name. It will

> *When Jesus came, the heavens were rent forever. Never before had sinful and common men seen the hosts of God and the landscape lit by dazzling splendor from heaven. Heaven's door had opened and light streamed across the earth. We need a personal relationship with this Personal God.*

cancel all invitations made to unclean spirits that open the doors to suppressions, heaviness and bondages from darkness. It will open up the avenue of the believer's Authority.

7. The Spirit of Wisdom: **Ephesians 1:17, "That the God of our Lord Jesus Christ, the Father of glory, may give to you the spirit of wisdom and revelation in the knowledge of Him."** Not only will the Spirit give us a knowledge of Jesus, but it will give us insight into His mind and what He is doing (1 Corinthians 2:6-16). The Holy Spirit is our teacher (John 14:26). The Mind of Christ is a divine process of thinking that is bestowed upon each of us the moment we are born again(2 Corinthians 2:12-16). This understanding for this supernatural gift of God (the Mind of Christ) is Isaiah 11:1-2:

These are the seven profound works that the Spirit will change in our lives as we walk into the fullness of God. If we allow Him to do these works in and through us, He will perfect us. As we seek to serve the Master and yield to these seven functions of the Spirit of God who will change us from glory to glory into the image of the son of God.

The Scriptures says: *"But without faith it is impossible to please Him, for he who comes to God must believe that He is, and that He is a rewarder of those who diligently seek Him."* (Hebrews 11:6 NKJV) Why aren't many believers walking in the glorious, because we aren't "diligently" seeking Him, the way that He desires and requires. The word "diligent" means, "Marked by persevering, painstaking effort." How many believers do we see taking great pains and paying the price to seek the Lord.

The Scripture says: *Seek ye the LORD while he may be found, call ye upon him while he is near*: (Is 55:6). Often we go to God to seek His hands; hands that give, hands that help, hands that bless, hands that protect, hands that heal, etc. There is nothing wrong with that, actually, God tells us in His Word to go to Him with our requests and that we do not have because we do not ask. There is nothing wrong with seeking God's blessing hands. The problem is that we spend a lot of time seeking God's hands so that we get blessed and we forget to spend seeking His face.

Moses said to the Lord, "See, You say to me, 'Bring up this people,' but You have not let me know whom You will send with me. Yet You have said, 'I know you by name, and you have also found grace in My sight.' Now, therefore, I pray You, if I have found favor in Your sight, show me now Your way, that I may know You, and that I may find favor in Your sight. Consider too that this nation is Your people."

And He said, "My Presence will go with you, and I will give you rest."

Then he said to Him, "If Your Presence does not go with us, do not bring us up from here. For how will it be known that I have found favor in Your sight, I and Your people? Is it not by Your going with us, so that we will be distinguished, I and Your people, from all the people who are on the face of the earth?"

The Lord said to Moses, "I will do this thing of which you have spoken, for you have found favor in My sight, and I know you by name."

Then Moses said, "I pray, show me Your glory."

Then He said, "I will make all My goodness pass before you, and I will proclaim the name of the Lord before you. I will be gracious to whom I will be gracious and will show mercy on whom I will show mercy." He said, "You cannot see My face, for no man can see Me and live."

Then the Lord said, "Indeed, there is a place by Me. You must stand on the rock. While My glory passes by, I will put you in a cleft of the rock and will cover you with My hand while I pass by. Then I will take away My hand, and you will see My back, but My face may not be seen (Ex. 33:12-23).

Oh what a glorious moment for Moses that he was able to see the glory of God as He passes over and how glorious will it be for each of us to be able to see that Glory as Moses did, if only we are filled with the same passion and hunger as Moses, It will be glorious indeed.

"He who dwells in the shelter of the Most High will abide in the shadow of the Almighty" (Ps. 91:1).

Did you know there is a place in God, a secret place, for those who want to seek Him. It is a literal place of physical safety and security that God tells us about in this psalm. Dwelling in the shelter of the Most High is the Old Testament's way of teaching faith. This gives us the most intense illustration of the very essence of a personal relationship with this Personal God.

II SAM 22:30

Is 10:27 And it shall come to pass in that day, that his burden shall be taken away from off thy shoulder, and his yoke from off thy neck, and the yoke shall be destroyed because of the anointing.

9 CONTENDING FOR BREAKTHROUGH

II SAM 22:30
For by thee I have run through a troop: by my God have I leaped over a wall.

When we are filled with the baptism of the Holy Spirit, we will be anointed with God's divine presence and this presence will produce mighty results. The overflowing of this presence is known as the anointing, in bible times known as virtue (Luke8:46)*'And Jesus said, Somebody, hath touched me: for I perceive that virtue is gone out of me'*

Acts 1:8 *'Ye shall receive power after the Holy Ghost come upon you'* indicates that with this infilling we are endued with power from high…For a breakthrough to take place in our walk with God in the spirit dimension, we need to press through into the supernatural.

(Mark 9:14-29) At the foot of the mountain, they found a great crowd surrounding the other disciples, as some religious leaders were arguing with them. The crowd watched Jesus in awe as he came toward them and they ran to greet him. When he came down from the mountain perhaps his face was glowing with Glory from heaven just as it happened to Moses when he came down from Mount Sinai. Jesus came down to chaotic scene in which he couldn't tell what his disciples and the religious leader were arguing. I believe these crowd were arguing on the method of casting out demons and the religious leader was using the disciples' failure to cast out the demons against Jesus legitimacy. Somewhere along this arguments, the actual demon possessed boy was lost in the shuffle as the disciples and the teachers argued. The master addressed the situation by asking the father 'If you believe all things are possible'. It was not the question whether if Jesus has the authority and the power to cast the demons out but rather if they had the faith to believe the impossible. No one in the crowd including the father of the lad displayed faith to release the supernatural.

When Jesus spoke the word, His word was in authority and the powers of hell recognize this kind of authority that goes with faith. Every time a word is spoken to someone faith must be present or else that word will fall to the ground as empty ineffective mere words without any results. When faith get itself attached to the authoritative word of God, it produces mighty results.

When everyone had left them and the lad returned back home with his father his disciples approached him and asked him privately, how they were not able to cast out the demons. Jesus opened up their understanding and gave them the key to unlocking heaven's treasure. It is by prayer and fasting that will produce such kind of authority and to release a supernatural breakthrough on someone's life.

Is 58:6 *'Is not this the fast that I have chosen? to loose the bands of wickedness, to undo the heavy burdens, and to let the oppressed go free, and that ye break every yoke?* Fasting is a necessary ingredient that will prepare the spirit man to step into the authority realm where the anointing will be released through faith. Many believers are able to pray long prayers but to put their flesh under subjection through fasting it is a difficult thing to do. Normally when we fast we get away from the crowd and spend days at the master's feet seeking after him.

At one time at my local assembly there was a lady that has come for few weeks to our church service and the moment she gets to the altar she would throw herself to the floor and wriggle and would manifest in a strange way. Some ladies tried to cast the spirit out but there would be a struggle and after a long time, this lady would return back home with such a heavy load.

As I was travelling on mission, the moment I got back they approached me and told me about the situation they were facing. The following weekend this lady turn up again at church and I directed some elderly women to take her to a room. I told everyone to keep out and only take few intercessors with me, as we prayed for her the demons manifested violently and became very aggressive. As I asked the demons, they spoke one after the other saying they are many, infact thousands were inside of her and called themselves as legion. We began to cast out these spirits and bands of spirit would come out at a time.

> *Someone needs to stand up with the power of God in their life and demonstrate that Jesus is not some dead, cold, figure hanging on a crucifix - the cross is empty, the tomb is empty, and Jesus is alive!*

Finally, when we got to the big man inside of her, this demon spoke in man's voice and refuse to go. As we called the name of Jesus for it to leave, that lady began to vomit green stuff from her and with a loud scream came out and on the way out as this spirit left through a glass door, when it passed through the glass door it broke the glass door in pieces. Nevertheless, that woman was delivered that day, not only delivered but we prayed her through the baptism of the Holy Ghost.

Once we cast out a demon from a possessed person, that house is empty and when the demon return the next day finding the house is clean, it will bring worse spirits than before and will take hold and possessed that individual that was delivered. (Luke 11:24-26)

We need to pray for them for the infilling of the Holy Spirit so that the house now is full of God's spirit and not empty anymore. From my early days, I've cast numerous of demonic spirit from people and every time a person is delivered, they will be prayed for, for the infilling of the Holy Spirit. This is not flamboyant ministry but a needed one. Only those who have prepared themselves in prayer and fasting and have close walk with the Lord will able to have an effective deliverance ministry.

When we receive such kind of anointing, it will set us apart for his service. It is not the question of, if God will use us for his kingdom as in the days of the apostles rather the question is can God trust us with such an anointing and can we be accountable to Him once we are endued with it.

We find in the scriptures that not only the priests such as Aaron and his sons were set aside for the service of God by having the anointing oil poured upon them but same happened with kings. (I Sam 16:13) *Then Samuel took the horn of oil, and anointed him in the midst of his brethren: and the Spirit of the* LORD *came upon David from that day forward.*

The anointing of oil is sanctification or setting apart of that person for God's sole purpose and service. We cannot be the same and return back to the earthly vocation and call. Yes we might have responsibility but we need to trust in Him who has called us out of darkness into His marvelous light and he is the perfect author and finisher of our faith. The anointing will sustain and keep us in a perfect place with God.

> *Sometimes the world will echo that we should not pray for the sick to be healed in the name of Jesus, because "it would raise false hopes." If we as believers do not practice what the Master passed down to us because some are not healed, then the same applies to medical doctors. After all, almost everybody in the cemeteries have seen a doctor first.*

Elijah found Elisha "while he was plowing with twelve pairs of oxen before him, and he with the twelfth." This seems to indicate that Elisha belonged to a family of considerable wealth. To obey the prophetic call would mean doing so at a considerable personal loss, financially speaking. It would mean counting the costs. It meant counting his financial security as loss and becoming a soldier of the Lord in the trenches of a tremendous spiritual conflict. But Elisha's responses in verses 20 and 21 of 1Kings19, shows us he was a man of faith who was willing to do just that. When someone is being touched and filled with the fullness of God and His Glory, they cannot be the same anymore. It will be as Paul's experience on the road to Damascus. This experience that changed Paul from a Pharisaic Jew to a Holy Ghost believer.

For the next three days, it was life changing experiences while he waited for his healing. The encounter and exposure to God's glory preceding with the healing of his sight opened up Paul's heart to search for God and for His high calling.

Once you have experienced the fullness of God in the Holy of Holies, there is no going back.

We had a young man from the Buddhist background that was acquainted with us and he wants to know the Lord and was visiting many churches while still living in sin. He would visit us at our home and on many occasions I would share with him the infilling and transforming power through the Holy Spirit. He was eager to be filled with God's power but he could not resist the sinful habits that had controlled his life. One particular day as his hunger for God grew and he was wanting more than religion he was taken into a bath tub to be baptized. As he went into the water and the glory of heaven beamed on him and all of a sudden he became as a child and cried out to God from the depth of his heart, confessed his sins and asked God to forgive him. Later he shared that God drew himself so close that he could feel the hand of Jesus embracing him the moment he stepped into the water. At this point, he was filled mightily with the infilling of the Holy Spirit and remained for a long time in the water late in the night speaking in tongues. Something broke loose as the glory touched him, he had no issue of giving up smoking, drinking and battling with other bad habits once he went into the water and was filled with God's spirit.

KNOWING THE WAYS OF GOD

Isaiah 55:8 *"For my thoughts are not your thoughts, neither are your ways my ways," declares the LORD.*

When we know and understand and are endowed with the foreknowledge of the ways of God we will be better apostles, prophets, evangelists, pastors and teachers and saints. The revelation of knowing God's hidden ways are not reserved for the few and to those in the ministry but to all those that seek and search after God with all their heart. Jer 29:13 *And ye shall seek me, and find me, when ye shall search for me with all your heart.*

When we need physical healing on our own body, knowing God's ways will increase our faith. God operates in the realm of faith when it comes to those who are saved and are his but God operates in the realm of grace and mercy to those who do not know him. Praying for healing toward others should not be a repetition act but it will be if the element of faith is missing. As one man of God said 'I'm not moved when I don't see things happen when I pray, I'm only moved by one thing that is the absence of Faith'.

At one time I was praying for an elderly man with severe bone condition in Nepal. At first nothing happened and he kept coming back for prayer and I refused to pray for him and told him to claim his healing. On the altar he lifted his hands and just did that, he started to claim his healing and suddenly a heat wave fell on him and his body was getting hot and he cried 'I feel hot all over my body' and then all the pain in his body vanished and he was healed at that moment. Many times when we pray for people that need healings and in the revival meetings, people

> *The greatest thing we can ever do for eternity is lead a human soul to the foot of the cross and see that soul transformed by the sound of the Master's voice, by the touch of His hand, By the glory of the greatest love story that has ever been told--that a man laid down His life for His friends*

that received their healing would testify that before they receive the healing their physical body would feel a heat sense. When the element of faith intermingle with the healing anointing in a particular place or in a service you can begin to expect a miracle is about to be birthed.

HOLDING ON TO YOUR HEALING

John 5:14 *Afterward Jesus found him in the temple, and said to him, "See, you have been made well. Sin no more, lest a worse thing come upon you."*

An individual that has been healed and set free need to be covered under the blood all the time, any open door for sin in his life will only invite back the spirit of infirmity that has hold on him earlier, infact the master proclaimed this way saying 'lest a worse thing come upon you. Once delivered and healed we need to guard our healing and not to lose it through sin and disobedience to God.

I was ministering to a sister at one time on the death bed in the hospital. She was battling with many issues and had lost all hope and the doctors had given up all hope on her. The Holy Spirit revealed that day that she will be healed and she will walk out of that hospital in 3 days' time and God will extend her life for another 10 more years but she need to surrender her life to the lord and give up her sinful habits and ways. That was what exactly happened, she walked out of that hospital in 3 days period to the amazement of the doctors in that hospital. But she battled with her sins and couldn't give up smoking and drinking. She stayed out from coming to church and the local pastor persuaded her many times to come to church and surrender her life.

> *Some churches are like flight-simulators on a grand exhibit. The student-pilot thinks he's flying realistically at 40,000 feet—yet he is bolted to the ground. All on the screen, but not on the scene.*

She refused and after 6 months later she was taken back to the same hospital for worse things had taken over her physical body and she died there in that hospital losing her healing and being lost.

When I was holding a revival meeting in Delhi, the capital city of India many years ago, we had a hall full of unbelievers from different parts of the city and during the prayer and altar session, God was present to meet these people. Many had come with affliction in their physical body as well those that were demon possessed. As soon God's presence fell in that place there were many that were possessed with demonic spirit who began to manifest violently. These demonic spirits were trying to hinder all those that have come for healing and also for salvation in that meeting. I had to give instruction to the elders to take these possessed people to a room and lock them up in a room until the service is over. Once the service concluded and the crowd left back home the elders brought out these people that were locked up to be prayed for. I asked them who they are and what is their agenda, the chief demon spoke out and said 'We were sent out from hell for the meeting today to stop all these people from getting saved and healed in their bodies" They further mentioned that every time someone is being filled with the Spirit of God or receive healing, they lose their hold on certain area on this earth that they are occupying. As I ask them how do you operate to stop this people they said 'It is through the mind of the people, we cast darts of doubts and these healings and salvation is not for them'

Later we cast out all the spirits from these people and prayed for them for the infilling of the Holy Spirit.

1Pet 5:8 *Be sober, be vigilant; because your adversary the devil, as a roaring lion, walketh about, seeking whom he may devour.*

But the devil often works in more subtle or hidden ways. When we think we can sin and get away with it, we're falling for the devil's lies. When we allow greed or jealousy or anger to overcome us, we're giving in to the devil's influence. When we think we don't need God and believe we can run our lives without Him, we've let our minds to be blinded by his deceptions. The Bible says that Satan works "in every sort of evil that deceives those who are perishing" (2 Thessalonians 2:10).

We must put on the armor of God, which includes the defensive weapons of truth, righteousness, gospel proclamation, faith, and salvation. We must also employ the offensive weapons of the sword of Scripture and prayer (Eph 6:11-18). These are the only means by which we may firmly stand against the enemy.

In that same meeting, there was one sister who had arthritis in her body for 13 years who received her healing on the first night and the moment she went back home doubt will invade her of her healing and on the next day we will find her at the altar praying for her healing again. On the third night, we had some that were facing this similar situation. The enemy was battling with these people and trying to keep them from receiving their complete healing. On that same night, the Lord brought the revelation of the ten lepers that were healed but only one could believe and return to Jesus to thank him for the healing that had taken place. I told the crowd that not only to have faith for their healing but to put action in their faith and to raise their hands and start to thank the Lord for their healing. As these people raised their hands and started to thank Jesus, we felt a thick cloud of glory that came in and the angels have step into that hall to join them in praise and thanks to Jesus. The chains of infirmities began to fell off their bodies and they received their healing and were delivered and never encountered the problem again.

There are few methods that the enemy uses to keep us from receiving our full healing and the biggest of all is 'doubt'. The thing that hurts the devil the most, is when a soul is suddenly changed by the saving power of God.

Healing comes in many forms, It may be instant or gradual, it may be complete or partial, it may be received through the operation of the gift of healing, through faith, through healing anointing. No matter how healing is administered it covers every sickness. Psalms 103:3 *Who forgiveth all thine iniquities; who healeth all thy diseases.*

God's healing power is limited only by the believers capacity to receive and retain it.

Why some lose their healings.

i) Those that are healed but not saved, Salvation is the seal and ground that keep the healing secure as a strong safe box that keeps the treasures. When the healing gift is in operation during a service many people receive their healing but failed to surrender their hearts to Jesus, they are not born of the water and the spirit. The gospel is more than healing, its more than deliverance, it's Salvation the biggest miracle. When a person is born again of the water and of the Spirit, they have access to the wisdom, knowledge, and power of almighty God! The Gospel is not an amendment to improve a human resolution. It is a complete document cancelling all debate and debts of sin and sickness, and declaring it an illegal gathering to find other means of salvation. Not matter how humble the Gospel preacher might be, effectively he is an officer of the crown speaking with authority from the Kingdom of God.

> *The Great Commission could never be carried out by any ordinary church. It called for fresh encounter with fire of Pentecost. The early church saw that it could not be carried out without the demonstration of God's Spirit. They began to ring the door-bell of heaven with prayer and fasting, ceaselessly and God stretch the heavens and step into their world.*

The miracle seed of healing and deliverance require good ground to grow on (Matt 13:4) says some seed fell on the way side and the fowls came and devoured them up. If you're not baptized in the water and the spirit and live a holy life, you're an open prey for the enemy. They will rob and devour your healing and blessings.

ii) Many are healed but ignorant of the word and faith, now faith cometh by hearing and hearing the word of God. The devil is going to come back after you have received your healing, deliverance and salvation and bombard you with so many darts of doubts, with every lie and symptoms he can muster. He will plant the seed of doubt and make you think the healing never took place in the first place. The only element that will ward away this attack is Faith, faith beyond any human understanding that holds to the word of God and His promises.

Faith is not what you have or what you possessed. A theological doctorate is not usually any help in the table of a surgeon. Faith has no mystique, nothing esoteric or rare. It is just common among the simple and childlike, ordinary everyday trustfulness. It is as good among humble people as among spiritual geniuses and religious giants. The mixed crowd that approached Jesus 'only believed' and the woman with an issue of blood for twelve years suffering 'only believed too', and their faith put their feet into the Supernatural breakthrough they were longing for.

Even ordinary faith produces outstanding people, though not all church members are notable examples of its galvanizing power. Some are still at the growth stage, where they declare they would go through fire and water for God. Paul and Silas in Philippi, sick with horribly mutilated backs, had a celebration meeting in the pitch dark prison, and then conducted a baptismal service through their faith.(James 1:3&4) *Knowing this, that the trying of your faith worketh patience. But let patience have her perfect work, that ye may be perfect and entire, wanting nothing.*

iii) Many that are healed were unable to resist the attack of the enemy. The enemy will bring many temptations that you will give in to sin and that will open up the door for sickness to return. Sin is a corrupted seed that will yield and

> *God is committed to fulfil His promise "I will build my church and the Gates of Hell will not prevail". Nobody can destroy what God builds not even most powerful demon in Hell. The works of the Cross and the pillars of the Spirit filled church is the immovable rock in the history of the roaring seas of mankind.*

grow up to destroy both physical and spiritual. Don't let the enemy get the foothold of your life. Eph 4:27 *Neither give place to the devil.* He that is in you is greater than he that is in the world, the enemy will only go as far you allow him to. The devil and the powers of Hell have no power and control over you 1Pet 5:8 *Be alert and of sober mind. Your enemy the devil prowls around like a roaring lion looking for someone to devour.* We are made victorious through His Word, Blood and Name.

A believer said to me at one time "I have a demon taunting me all the time in my head and I cant sleep." I asked "Are you a born again believer?" She nodded yes. Suddenly, the Holy Spirit light up a revelation inside of me and I asked "do you know that flies love to sit on a cold fire grill, Get the fire and heat of the Holy Spirit into your life and your devil-problem is gone forever. When your "stove" is hot and some fly approaches, it suddenly senses the hotness and sharply veers it away. We are protected by "a wall of fire" the fire of the Holy Ghost.

iv) Many that are healed fail to keep in line with the word of God will never put sickness and diseases back to you but when you step out of the order and will of God, you are vulnerable and unprotected. You break the covering and the hedge of protection that God has put around your life. It gives an easy access to the enemy to afflict you again with its sting of sickness and death. But as long the blood of Jesus covers you, no devil in Hell is powerful enough to break that barrier.

v) Many that are healed failed to see themselves as being healed. When God touches your physical body He sees you healed and completely whole. Don't let the unreal physical world dim your view of the regeneration in the spiritual realm.

vi) Many that are healed failed to profess and confess with their mouth the healing received. They don't even step out to testify of their healing to others. Once you have caught the vision of your healing let your mouth be filled with praise thanksgiving and testimony that will affirm your healing.

Rev 12:11 And they overcame him by the blood of the Lamb, and by the word of their testimony

Acts 1:8 But ye shall receive power after the Holy Ghost is come upon you; and ye shall be witnesses unto Me both in Jerusalem, and in all Judea and in Samaria, and unto the uttermost part of the earth."

10 RECEIVING AND RELEASING

It has been 400 years since God's people had heard a word from the Lord. As in the days just before Samuel's ministry a word from the Lord was rare in those days, vision and prophecy was infrequent. (1Sam 3:1)

And the child Samuel ministered unto the Lord before Eli. And the word of the Lord was precious in those days; there was no open vision.

All these while long a faithful remnant among God's people was praying that he would fulfill His longstanding promise to the world through the Messiah. Then suddenly without any advance notice, God broke the silence and into history, announced and what he was about to do through the birth of John the Baptist as the forerunner of the messiah.

This forerunner went forth dressed in camel's skin and was found in the caves of Jerusalem meditating the Torah. His Staff and His rod were is companion dressed in a rugged way but His voice echoed *'Prepare Ye the way of the Lord for the Kingdom of God is at Hand'.*

He was preaching about the soon coming King that is about to appear in the scene and when Jesus came he proclaimed *'The Spirit of the Lord is upon me, because he hath anointed me to preach the gospel to the poor; he hath sent me to heal the brokenhearted, to preach deliverance to the captives, and recovering of sight to the blind, to set at liberty them that are bruised'*

When God brings revival in our days it is because His people which are called by His name have humbled themselves, repent and die to their works of the flesh and every desire of the world and flesh, seek His face continually and allowing Him to fill you completely with his spirit and walking in the order of the spirit of God. God has promised us to be mighty conquerors for Him and not a wimpy Christian sitting somewhere around the corners of this earth waiting for the Lord to return. The scripture declared that Ye shall receive power after the Holy Ghost come upon you and Ye Shall be witnesses unto him.

HIS POWER AVAILETH TO US THROUGH BIRTH

When we open up to the divine revelation of God and remove all the garbage's in the flesh then we can understand how mightily God can take us on the journey of His spirit. Embark on the things that appear and bring the things that do not appear to prominence.

On the richness of God's Glory, Jabez knew God is more than His wants and there are divine principles that he need to embark on, He cried 'Enlarge Me Oh God' 1 Chron 4:10

And Jabez called on the God of Israel, saying, *Oh that thou wouldest bless me indeed, and enlarge my coast, and that thine hand might be with me'*. When Prophet Joel proclaimed through the vision that the days are coming when God is going to enlarge His people through the spirit he said *'In the last days God will pour out His spirit upon all flesh'*. All fullness dwell in Him, we all have received a grand infilling and the fullness of his presence and power.

> *When we begin believing and are planted in the name of Jesus, we are not just "believers." We are re-positioned; it is a spiritual shift. We are not just members in some church; we are placed INSIDE of what that name represents. His name is Power, His name is Deliverance, His name Salvation; His name is All in. all.*

In weakness, strength, poverty, sickness, death is this divine glory. It is a flame of fire. It may burn in our bones, it may move in every tissue, it may bring you out forcibly into his plan until his purpose is fulfilled in each of us.

It will take nine months to bring us forth into this world after we are conceived but it only takes a moment to beget us as sons of the living God the minute we are filled with his Spirit.

THE PRICE OF THE HIGH CALLING OF GOD

While I was in Tibet ministering, I was so moved to meet a young lady who has totally given herself to the Lord, by birth she was brought up in a Buddhist family. At the age of 12 Jesus appeared to her in a dream and revealed himself to her. She has forsaken everything and followed Jesus, her family began to beat her up and torture her daily; physically abused and threatening to kill her if she didn't forsake her faith in Jesus. They would lock her in a room for many months and beat her up, her uncle would visit her and would coax into giving her a lot of money if only she deny Jesus and follow after their Buddhism faith. In those days God would visit her in that room and where no evangelist, preacher is available and allowed into that terrirory, God filled her mightily with his spirit. She was taken up in a vision to the throne of God and would lost herself in the presence of the Lord for many hours. When the family could not change her belief, finally they gave her food and filled it with poison to kill this young girl. The Lord revealed it to her and she ate in obedience and God spared her life, she was not harmed by the poison. They drove her from their village and country because they couldn't do anything to change her mind. But God raised her up to be a mighty vessel to raise many death people, many Tibetan monks were healed through her prayers and the revival fire spread through the country because when she got hold of Jesus and was filled with his spirit, she was transformed as a mighty conqueror.

The Holy Spirit is the revelator and the working power in New Testament church. He is the very essence of a believer's faith, brought to us by the truth. Jesus said Ye shall know the truth and the truth shall set you free There is no Christianity without the working of the spirit of God. He is not an accessory, but the very substance and the core of what we believe and live. Christianity is a supernatural transformation by the hand of the spirit. A non-supernatural gospel and a non-supernatural church is only an empty shell.

SET APART FOR GOD

John the Baptist, the prophet, teacher and man of God used to spark revival wherever he goes. He was set apart unto God while he was in his mother's womb, God chose this prophet to be distinctly different from the religious system and culture around him even from the local religious authorities during his time. Rather than being control by wine he chooses to be under the leadership of the spirit of God. Eph 5:*18 And be not drunk with wine, wherein is excess; but be filled with the Spirit.* He was to go before the Lord in the power and might of Elijah(Luke1:17) to turn back many of the children of Israel to the creator. He was filled with God's spirit from his mother's womb even before he was birthed into this world. He was separated, chosen, filled and was ready to pay the price that will cost his very own head to Herod.

> *On the richness of God's Glory Jabez knew God is more than His wants and there are divine principles that he need to embark on, He cried 'Enlarge Me Oh God' And God did Enlarged Him and erected a monument that testify of His goodness throughout the generations.*

When God began to anoint you in a greater way and the authority of His Kingdom on your life, you are accountable for that gifting and anointing. Every great gifts and unction from above require a greater accountability. It's one thing to be anointed and another to be always under the subjection of the spirit of God that we don't want to step out of the order of God. This same gifting and anointing can turn against us to destroy us if we fall away. We need the hedge of the fruit of the spirit to always keep our feet orderly in our walk with him. 1Sam 16:14

says, *"The Spirit of the LORD had departed from Saul, and an evil spirit from the LORD tormented him."* First, the evil spirit was allowed by God to harass Saul. Ultimately, all created things are under God's control. It is likely that this evil spirit was part of God's judgment upon Saul for his disobedience. Saul had directly disobeyed God on two occasions (1 Samuel 13:1-14; 15:1- Therefore, God removed His Spirit from Saul and allowed an evil spirit to torment him. Likely, Satan and the demons had always wanted to attack Saul.

When God uses us as a mighty vessel for his kingdom we are the biggest threat to the devil's kingdom as we will cause much damage to him and his powers and the demonic power will be assigned to attack us from every angle but because we are covered under that anointing and the blood of Jesus, those spirits can't touch us, however, the minute we fall away from grace, we become open to every attack of the enemy and the same gifts that is in on our life will turn against us. Many mighty man that have been used greatly had fallen due to sin, their gifts might seem to be in operation for a while even after they had backslided but eventually, their sin will find them out and they will be destroyed. We must never have confident in our gifting neither in the anointing that is upon our lives but on the Master always, having a deep closer relationship with him. Only the deep relationship with Him will guarantee every success of our ministry and the continuous operation of the anointing. We are the heir to all the promises and God's treasure house because it's a heritage passed down from the apostles. We are made more than overcomers because we embraced the truth and the truth set us free (John 8:32).

The root principle of all this divine overcoming life is in Jesus alone, when you're grafted deeply in him. You may draw millions to the foot of the cross through that Love of Calvary.

GREATER ANOINTING DEMANDS A GREATER SACRIFICE

A greater anointing and authority in the spirit demands a greater sacrifice. There is a price to pay in order to obtain the crown of glory and sometimes it requires everything of us. God requires everything from us without any reservation. (Luke 12:48) *For unto whomsoever much is given, of him shall be much required: and to whom men have committed much, of him they will ask the more.*

If you desire to be taken to a greater anointing, you must be willing to pay a greater sacrifice, walk the extra mile, carry the difficult cross and be willing to crucify the flesh in order for the spirit man to rise. Those who will carry this anointing because of its cost, must put their trust in God. It is God and only him that has called you into this journey and He will complete it when you submit yourself all the time at the foot of the cross.(1Thes 5:24) *Faithful is he that calleth you, who also will do it.*

> *When God uses us as a mighty vessel for his kingdom we are the biggest threat to the devil's kingdom. Christians may look tame, but so does an electric cable - till you touch it.*

A few years back when we step foot into Nagaland a tribal nation that has accepted the Lord and the truth, we travelled quite extensively into the jungle area without proper road system and through the mountain terrain for hours and hours. Sometimes it will take sixteen hours before we reach a village, but when we arrived at a certain village early hour of the morning the people were waiting eagerly to hear the word of God. We would go into the service where the people already are waiting since 4am in the morning with prayer and fasting and just with a tribal drum, they would lift their heart and soul to the Lord in deep worship. No choir, no modern music, no worship leader, just them and the Lord. Many a times I would experience as I'm standing in the upper room in Jerusalem back in the apostles time, where the mighty rushing wind of God would blow in with fire. People would fall prostrate on the mud floors and remain there for hours in God's presence engulfed in the glory. When we leave the place no one was sick any more, no one was without the spirit for all have been filled and all have been healed. No one want to leave these meeting place as there is no time limit for the service schedule, everyone was just waiting and receiving and been lifted in the glorious presence of Jesus, sometimes the glory of God is so mighty and thick that we could not minister just weep and weep and drink from the cup of joy from heaven. Angels and the host of heaven would join us and we will feel the brush of wings and the covering of those angels wings on us while we are taken into the glory place.

We were taken to a neighborhood where some of these believers had become martyrs to the other tribal groups in a particular village. As they were taken deep into the jungle and were asked to deny their faith in Jesus, these saints just kneeled on the ground one by one and watched their friend being beheaded. They rather being killed for the name of Jesus than to refute their love and faith for the lord. They have so much of the kingdom of God in them that this world is just a temporary abode as they look daily for the return of the Lord in much expectation.

The Great Commission in Matt 28 :19 ushers us to the mission of the Lord. It is the reason for a churches and the believers to live. Concerned only with itself, the church is purposeless and dead in God's eyes and harmless to the kingdom of hell. Faith only operates when it's yoked together with the purpose of God that is to seek and save the lost with His truth.

David was a mere shepherd boy when God found him and the kingly anointing was placed on his life. When prophet Samuel came looking for David, he was missing at home, he was in the field attending to his father's sheep. Lazy and slothful servants will not inherit anointing from God. It takes a real man and woman who will roll up their sleeves and get their hands dirty in the field to win souls. When God's eyes turn toward you, are you busy in the field for souls?

PROTECTING GOD'S PRECIOUS ANOINTING

1 Thes 5:19-22 *Do not quench the Spirit. Do not despise prophecies. Test all things; hold fast what is good. Abstain from every form of evil.*

Protecting the flame and anointing that The Lord has placed within you is difficult when you are bombarded with self-centered and ungodly messages in the society. Our culture promotes a lifestyle of gain and revenge over giving and grace. Integrity is a forgotten priority in leadership and roles in the public eye. But integrity is a major priority in the eyes of God, it feeds the anointing of God in our lives. Pride is a weapon of mass destruction, when placed alongside with the anointing. Hence the anointing of God is designed merely to equip us for service and to reach out to the lost. Everything accomplished through it, needs to bring glory to the Lord only If you want The Lord to move in a powerful way in you and through you, live with integrity no matter who is watching alone or with a crowd. Smother yourself in the Word... pray without ceasing. Guard your heart. Protect your anointing. It is precious. Its favor is your most powerful covering. Through it, you can accomplish everything God has appointed for you. Without it, it's all about you.

> *The Holy Spirit is the New Testament Revelator and Power through the ordinary men. He is the very essence of the believer's faith, brought to us by the Truth. There is no Christianity without him. He is not an accessory, but the very substance of our Salvation and the end time move.*

RELEASING WHAT YOU RECEIVE

1 TIMOTHY 4:14
Do not neglect the spiritual gift within you, which was bestowed on you through prophetic utterance with the laying on of hands by the presbytery.

We need to RELEASE that Anointing that God has placed in our Lives. That means to allow God and His anointing to work in our lives and to work through our lives. If you want to release water from a tap, you have to turn the tap.

If you want to release a balloon from your hand, you have to open your grip from the balloon.

When we opened up ourselves to the Holy Spirit to flow through us, he will flow through us into other vessels. God doesn't want His vessels to be like a lake that doesn't flow out but rather a river, a living river. The only way God can increase what you already have is when you step out and give to others, when you lay hands and pray for the sick, when you lay hands and pray for someone to receive the Holy Spirit. When you step out in faith the river is ready to flow from you and there will be a demonstration of the works of the spirit through the anointing. The consuming passion and work of the spirit were 'to seek and to save the lost world.' Jesus was never just a miracle worker. It was not for some social good works—just to feed multitudes—turn the water into wine and draw out a coin from the fish mouth but for the redemption of man. That was his passion any desire of 'greater works' has to be in line with the master's burden, to save the lost.

Acts 8:18 *And when Simon saw that through laying on of the apostles' hands the Holy Spirit was given, he offered them money.* Simon was a sorcerer and he must have witnessed hundreds if not thousands of supernatural manifestation through the dark world but when Peter and John had a greater mightier demonstration of the anointing and through their laying of hands not only did the people received the Holy Spirit but there must be more as this sorcerer saw, he witnessed the power of God through the anointing that flows from the life of these apostles.

> *The word Gospel does not mean reformation, decoration or renovation, but liberation transformation and transition. Its no longer we that live but Christ in Us the Hope of Glory.*

When we were holding revival meeting in Varanasi India, many people came and many were from the Catholic background. The Catholic Bishop gave us their premises to hold these meeting as we could not find a place since the Hindu religious movement learned that we will be there, they shut every door for the venue of the meeting. As faith rise in those meeting through many miracles that took place the catholic group step out to be prayed for and God sent the heavenly rain and filled them all with His spirit. Among them was a politician from that area and God already dealt with his heart when He was healed from spinal injury in that meeting, he step out and God filled him with the Holy Ghost. Then this politician came and said 'What will I do? God has dealt with me but I must have a foundation. Will you spend time with me? "Yes, of course, I will "Then as we went with him God broke his fallow ground and this Indian politician was going back to his Indian conditions with a new order. He had left a practice there and told me what a great practice he had as a politician. He was ready to go to practice to preach of Jesus of Nazareth now.

If you have lost your hunger and thirst for God and do not have a cry for more of Him, you're missing your purpose. Your hunger and thirst must come from deep within and can be fulfilled by God alone. He wants to give us the vision of the price ahead that is higher and purer compare to anything. If you ever stopped along the way in your journey seeking him more, begin again under the refining light and power of heaven. And while he brings you to your consciousness of your own frailty and to the brokenness of spirit, your faith will lay hold of Him and all the divine resources. His light and compassion will be manifested through you and He will send the Rain.

Matt 10:8 Heal the sick, cleanse the lepers, raise the dead, cast out devils: freely ye have received, freely give.

CPSIA information can be obtained
at www.ICGtesting.com
Printed in the USA
FFOW03n1948030717
37452FF